Out of the Ashes

A Wounded Daughter's Diary (Book 1)

Tyra Hodge

Deanna Wilson

Copyright © 2017 Deanna Wilson

For more information, go to
https://tyradhodge.blogspot.com/

Version: 2.0.0 (Read more). Published by Hodge Publishing Press (Conroe, Texas). 17615 Linda Lane Conroe, Texas 77306

No part of this e-book may be reproduced, stored, or transmitted in any form or by any means including mechanical or electronic without prior written permission from the author.

While the author has made every effort to ensure that the ideas, statistics, and information presented in this eBook are accurate to the best of his/her abilities, any implications direct, derived, or perceived, should only be used at the reader's discretion. The author cannot be held responsible for any personal or commercial damage arising from communication, application, or misinterpretation of information presented herein.

Out of the Ashes

Table of Contents

Introduction: Purpose of Writing this Book

And the Winner of the Pity Party Award is ...

Daddy Issues: What It *Really* Means

Club Life: When Partying All Night Long Seemed like a Good Idea

What You Need to Know about Strippers

Once Bitten, but Never Shy

Missing All the Turns

Walking Dead

The Baby Blues: What It's Really Like Being Pregnant

Next Stop: Wichita Falls

The Call

Back to School, Back to Life

The Turning Point

The Gruesome Twosome

Job Hunt vs. Husband Hunt

A Marriage Made in Hell

God's Purpose: What He Really Wanted from Me

Good Things Come to Those Who Wait

Best Job Ever

The Birth of Some New Ideas

The Second-Best Year Ever

Epilogue

About the Author

About This Edition

Introduction: Purpose of Writing this Book

Have you ever watched a horror movie and felt as though you could see the villain lurking behind the door or outside the window? You probably found yourself yelling at the screen, "Get away from the door!" as you tried to warn the person of the danger that awaits them. You can clearly see that – if only the damsel would have picked up the bat she just tripped over, she would have an adequate chance of defending herself.

Instead, she walks right through that door unarmed and unprepared. As I look back on my life to write this book, I feel as though I am in a similar kind of movie. This time though, the foolish movie character walking unarmed and unprepared into one perilous situation after another is ... ME! All the pain I went through, the people that I hurt and the pain that I caused ... looking back, now I can clearly see how the dangers approached. I was often unequipped to deal with these situations, but at other times, I simply did not use the tools and training that I had. Either way, I fell right into the traps set for me by the most dangerous of all villains, Satan.

However, as I look back and see myself walking into those traps, I realize now that I was not alone: the loving hand of my heavenly Father was guiding me back to Him throughout my long and difficult journey. It can be distressing to retell the story of how my life went up in flames, but I hope that sharing it will help the others who are struggling with their own path. Perhaps, my story inspires you to rise from the ashes – stronger and wiser. Perhaps, my story will be just the thing that helps them rise from the ashes – stronger and wiser.

1. And the Winner of the Pity Party Award is ...

In senior year of high school, I read Nathaniel Hawthorne's *The Scarlet Letter*. From the moment I met the book's main character, Hester Prynne, I felt connected — both to her and her story. If you recall, her punishment for committing adultery was to wear a scarlet "A" on her outfits. I felt that our stories began to intertwine like yarn being handled by a toddler. As her fate was branded, so was the visualization of my own future. Despite the fact that our sins had engulfed us, our struggles will forever be remembered as strength.

Hawthorne could have never known that Hester Prynne would be a premonition of the corporeal depravity of a young girl's indiscretions. My own indiscretions. Everyone has been a victim of their own thoughtless actions now and then, however, one mishap in our existence can adjust or readjust the treads of our timeline and our existence.

For as long as I can remember, my life has been nothing but strenuous. Have you ever felt as if, right from the beginning, someone was purposely setting you up for the worst day of your life? That no matter how hard you try, nothing goes right, and everything that seems bad just keeps getting worse? Now imagine feeling that way not just for a couple of days, but for *thirty years*!

The first memory I have is about living in the beautiful state of New Jersey. I was born in Vineland, New Jersey with my pleasantly plump caregiver. We lived in a townhome – perfect for running up and down the stairs. The townhome was yellow on the outside with a playground right in the middle of the cul-de-sac. My mom had four boys and me. We were a handful. We were always running in and out of the house until my mom just left us outside until dinner time. My mom was an even-tempered woman who did her best to take care of us all by herself. We were as happy as could be, not knowing the difference between rich and poor. We did not get hugs and kisses, but we did get a couple of swats every now and then for running inside the house. Well, not everybody got swats. Usually, just the boys, for setting such a bad example for me. My out was my "yes momma" and a smile.

I was three years old when I was taken from my house in the middle of the night. It was a man and a woman. A black woman and a white man.

At the age of three, I did not understand anything about kidnapping, but I knew what these strangers were doing was a scary thing. I should have screamed when I felt someone grab me from my crib. The townhouse had only a couple of bedrooms, so I slept in a white baby crib in the small downstairs kitchen. The room had no windows, so it was usually dark; my crib sat across the stove by the back door.

What were they doing? And why? I was too afraid to scream. And it took me even longer to understand their motive.

On the drive (which seemed to take forever), I asked, "Where is my mom?" My face scrunched up in my frustration. The couple looked at each other and then, the white man spoke: "Deanna, this *is* your mother." The two of them looked convinced they were doing the right thing.

I was caught off guard by the fact that the man with the long hair even knew my name.

"Where is my mom? Take me back to my mom!" I decided it was time to use my bratty voice. Many years later, I realize that I must have sounded like a brat.

"Deanna, this is your mom", the man repeated. He didn't get frustrated with me even when I started to cry. His voice was almost soothing.

"Tell her," the man directed the lady kidnapper.

The woman turned to look at me in the back seat. "Deanna, my name is Anna Mae, I'm your mother. The lady you were living with is your aunt, my sister. She was taking care of you. I'm home now and I came to get you."

The official story was that my mother had gotten pregnant with me in her senior year of high school. She was without direction and alone. After some guidance from her sister, she finished high school and then, she was forcibly conscripted into the navy. Her sister assured her that I would be completely taken care of.

God has a way of always being right on time. If my mother would have left me where I was, my life would have taken a different course, and many things would have been different – most likely, things would have been worse. God saw fit to redeem me out of a bad situation by moving me back with my mother and saving me from additional abuse.

Later, when I was five, I visited my aunt's house again, but I dreaded it. I could not face being teased and humiliated by the boys again. I did not want to have to explain. But my mother wanted me to show her exactly what the boys had done. All I could manage to say was, "The boys were trying to make me have a baby."

I could not explain it right, probably because I did not want to have to explain what was happening to me. And besides, I was just five. Was it any surprise that a 5-year-old child would have trouble explaining that she had been put through inappropriate sexual situations? I was humiliated and embarrassed. I wished there was a way to take back my disclosure because I was just sent back over to my aunt's house. There were times I hated the other children. At just five years old, I knew hate. To not feel nasty and gross, I wanted them to care for me like friends, and I hated them for failing to be my protectors and not becoming my predators.

Growing up, I was afraid of hell and of God. I felt he was merciless and unforgiving. I spent a lot of time alone, talking to myself. This habit of conversing with myself is something I kept doing even as an adult. When I felt alone, I would escape into my own imaginary world, a place within my own self, so I did not have to feel and be alone. In this world which I created for myself, I was the center of attention. This world – my world – was perfect; everyone in it loved and cared for me.

2. Daddy Issues: What It Really Means

Daddy issues ... daddy issues. It's all over the talk shows and regularly appears in pop culture. Lawyers use this as an excuse to try to get criminals off. The problem with daddy issues is that they can sometimes give people a warped image of our one true father: God.

My own father situation left me with quite a few Daddy Issues, and they, in turn, affected my relationship with God. I have a biological father who chose not to make himself available to me as I grew up. This hurt a lot, especially as a teenager. But, when I was little, I did have a stepdad, and he was proud of me. He loved to take me everywhere. He would take me along to get his hair cut, to the park, to hang out with his friends, and even to strip clubs.

At the strip clubs, the women seemed to know him. I did think it was strange that he took me there to hang out. It was called a Go-Go Bar. If my mother had known this was where he spent his time, and that he had taken his 5-year-old daughter along, she would have certainly been angry. In retrospect, I realize that he used me as an excuse to get out of the house. He didn't want my mom to interrogate him about where he was going. So, he took me to help his cover story. He took me everywhere. Whatever his reasoning, the fact that he was not ashamed of me despite him being a white, made me proud. Strip clubs aren't the best place for a father-daughter quality time, but I was just happy to be getting his attention.

Although certain things about my stepfather were normal and positive, there was another side to him that was not so fun. Nearly every weekend, he would get drunk and get angry about something. Sometimes, he became so angry that he ripped apart things in our Virginia apartment. When he acted like this, my mother and I had little choice but to leave, and after he apologized, we would inevitably return.

One night, he had come home drunk and my mother wanted to leave. He then picked me up by the throat and told her that if she left, he would slit my throat. He had a pocketknife to the tender part of my throat; I could feel the sharp blade pricking at my neck. The sharp blade was bad enough, but I was also losing consciousness from the way he had me suspending in the air, his hand crushing my throat. Hanging there on the wall, I tried to squeeze out, "Daddy, please." I was so scared that he would cut me. I wasn't really afraid of dying – just of being stabbed. I was imagining the bloody mess that would have been everywhere.

"Leon, don't!" my mom screamed. "Please put her down!"

Weeping, my mother fell to her knees in complete surrender. Tears were also streaming down my face. "I won't leave. I won't leave!" my mother cried. "Just put her down."

After he finally let me down, I crumpled to the floor, light-headed, bruised, and gasping for air.

After that, my stepdad continued to drink and smoke his marijuana. He only seemed to get wasted on Fridays, probably because it was payday. He would always come home late, and if my mom was upset, he would hit a wall, break a door, smash a chair ... something. This was always his response to my mom's confrontations. He wasn't a cruel man by nature though. The alcohol just turned him either into an abusive person or a playful one. I never knew which one we would get.

There was another time I had gotten in trouble for something (I do not remember for what exactly). I was six years old. Whatever it was, my crying irritated my stepdad. He yelled at me to shut up, but I couldn't. I was too upset. He began to pace beside me whispering "shut up, shut up." My inability to stop only aggravated him more. His pacing grew faster as he grabbed the roots of his hair. In a sequenced swoop, he picked me up and threw me to the floor. He took the sharp tip of his boot and jammed it into my side. I screamed out in pain. He screamed out of shock too, as he just started to realize the pain he had just inflicted. My dad fell to his knees beside me and pleaded for forgiveness. "I'm so sorry, I am sorry." I knew he was sorry, but that didn't change the pain I felt in my ribcage for weeks. I never told my mom only because he begged me not to tell her, and his apology seemed very earnest as he began to cradle and rock me in his arms.

Even now, I wonder why I have never told my mom about this episode. At that moment, I had decided that I so wanted my stepdad to love me and knew this could be a secret we could share.

One night, I stayed up with my dad all night while he was drinking. We pretended that we were taking the Lord's supper. I broke up the little pieces of white bread and placed everything onto my little china set plates which I had laid out on the coffee table. In lieu of wine, my dad provided the beer. I was enjoying his company that night. We had pulled all-nighters before together. I did not seem to mind his drinking. He was always fun when it was just the two of us. Suddenly, my dad fell back into his favorite reclining chair. I thought he was fooling around, but he just lay on the chair with his eyes rolled back. I took the beer out of his hand and laid it on the table because it was spilling. The can was almost empty when I set it on the table. He had gone quiet. It was as if all the sound had escaped the room. I knew something was wrong. "Daddy," I said, shaking him gently. "Wake up, wake up." All I could see were the whites in his eyes and an almost ghostly look of shock. When I could not wake him, I went to get my mother.

"Mom, wake up!"

"Deanna go back to bed," my mother groaned, waving her hand in the air as if shooing away a fly.

"Mommy, Daddy won't wake up. He fell back in his chair and won't wake up. His eyes are open."

It was an unwritten rule that I never woke my parents, especially on weekends. I stood there for a moment until my mother finally realized that my persistence was out of character. She hurried to the next room and started shaking my stepdad.

"Leon, Leon!" she started crying, and her voice became unstable. "Baby please, don't do this". As her fear began to unravel, all I could do was — back away into the closest corner and squat. But he would not wake. My mom called the hospital. But by the time the ambulance arrived, my dad was already dead. The time on the clock had not changed; had all the clocks in the house stopped working, or had time stopped?

Although my stepdad wasn't perfect, I still loved him so much. His death was difficult for me. After he died, I always imagined that he was not really gone. I hoped that it was just a government conspiracy and that one day, he would show up in our lives. But he was dead, dead, dead … and what little attention he had given me also died with him. I loved my stepfather, and I believe he loved me back in his own way.

My stepdad's funeral was held at the Arlington National Cemetery, however, his body was eventually buried in Indiana in a separate funeral arranged by his family. For days after my dad's death, the stopped clocks in the house remained unfixed. On that second night, I could have sworn I saw his shadow lingering next to my bedroom closet. I could not explain such a phenomenon, but this would not be the only time such mysteries had occurred to me.

After my stepdad died, my mom began to go to church. Also, she chose to stay single. There would be no more abusive men in her life. Still, after seeing what my mother had gone through, I had unconsciously absorbed and internalized the pattern that abusive relationships tended to have: the vicissitudes of disappointment and pain and forgiveness.

Various studies in journals which conclude that parents are an important influence in their children's lives are no joke. They are preaching the truth. Having a good set of parents to look up to for morals and guidance is one of the biggest blessings anybody could ever wish for. I sometimes think of my mother and what she must have gone through, just for putting up with an abusive partner.

Not having a father figure in my life would sometimes make me think of Pearl, from *The Scarlet Letter*. Although I mainly identified with Hester, at times, I also identified with her illegitimate daughter Pearl. Neither Pearl nor I knew of an earthly father, just a heavenly one.

3. Club Life: When Partying All Night Long Seemed like a Good Idea

I began going to clubs with friends when I was 22. It was all so exciting and new. For the first time in my life, I was getting lots of attention from boys. Boys were talking to me and flirting. I felt almost attractive, especially now that I had discovered the hair weave.

I didn't get much attention growing up. I came from a big family, and after my mom became widowed, I was often overlooked and ignored. My mom worked long hours as a police officer to support us. As a result, she had limited ability to spend one-on-one time with each individual child.

Since I was the oldest, household chores usually fell on me. I was a responsible teenager in most regards, but not when it came to academics. School was definitely not for me. I had been held back twice in elementary school, and every year up until eighth grade, I was in danger of being held back again.

Suddenly receiving so much attention at the club was a refreshing change; it was also something I wasn't used to. It made the new club scene seem wonderful and exciting, like a drug I couldn't get enough of. Guys were truly interested in me (or so I thought). Little did I know that they were more interested in what they could get from me, and neither of those things included a handshake or a dance routine. My already weak self-esteem made me easily give in to their needs. And when they got what they wanted from me, they just moved on to the next piece of meat. I didn't care because I was finally getting the attention I craved.

At first, I went out once a week. But then, I started to go out more often until it was four nights a week. One night at the club, a girl asked me, "Are you a dancer?"

"I took a few lessons when I was younger," I said.

"No, girl, I am talking about topless."

I wasn't so sure what to say, so I simply stammered a no. I was even embarrassed that she asked. As she kept talking, I realized that the girl meant it as a compliment.

"Well, I'm Renee, and I bet you could make a lot of money," she explained.

That got my attention. I had been waiting tables at a restaurant and not making a lot of money. I could barely afford a place to live. So, when Renee said she could help me figure out a way to end my monetary troubles, I had to listen. Later, I wondered if I would still have responded positively if Renee hadn't been so persistent. She began calling every day to see if I wanted to meet up again.

It took her just a couple more calls and soon enough, we were hitting the club together. We became close. One day, Renee got the idea that we should get an apartment together with another friend Blanca.

I had absolutely no problems with that. It actually piqued me. Can you picture it? Blanca and Renee did all the leg work in finding something. A week later, I received a phone call from Renee saying they had found the perfect apartment. Three single women living together in a very spacious apartment across the street from our favorite club, J. Larkins. It was going to be the best year ever! It was great living with two other women who loved to live life to the fullest. Our after parties were epic.

After about a month of rooming with my girls (that's what I called them), their behavior started to seem a little … odd. There were many times when Blanca and Renee were alone in a room together, talking with the door shut. I began to wonder what they were talking about. I was afraid they were talking about me. It began to piss me off. One day, I decided to just walk in and there they were – knelt on the floor, sniffing white powder from straws.

"Do you want some?" Blanca asked. I just stared at them with my mouth agape in astonishment.

"No, thanks," I said. I could see they were very nervous about what I would think. I was shocked because I had never seen real cocaine before. My fight or flight response kicked in and I quickly left the room.

Anyway, I tried pushing the entire incident to the back of my mind. Later that night at the club, the two of them were feeling real lovey-dovey.

Renee kept saying, "I am wiggin. I am wiggin girl," with her eyes rolling back in her head. She seemed very happy.

I asked, "What is wiggin?" I felt stupid saying the word out loud.

Completely taken aback by my question, Renee looked at me as if I just asked the strangest question in the History of Strange Questions.

She laughed and said, "You don't know what wiggin is? You've heard of ecstasy, right?"

"Nope," I said.

"You have to try it," she said. "It's not a hard drug."

"Na, girl I don't do drugs." I always remained firm in that stance.

"You can't get addicted to it because it is a pill."

"Really?"

"You'll love it. I'll get you one. Trust me, it's better to do it with a group."

I had to admit, Renee's confident attitude convinced me that the chances of getting addicted were small. Like most people who have never tried drugs, I worried about getting addicted. But if what Renee said was true, what did I have to lose?

Nothing!

I eventually gave in and tried it. I would like to tell you it was a bad experience, but unfortunately, I can't. It was great! The comedown, however, was horrible.

With stimulants like cocaine and ecstasy, your serotonin and dopamine levels get higher than normal, and it gives you the same kind of feeling as being in love. When the body starts to come down, it wants the peak again. So, a person will dose themselves again, though it is nearly impossible to regain the original high. With each comedown, the low feels worse than before because you have interfered with the normal functioning of serotonin producers and receptors in your brain.

The comedown is what encourages people to do whatever it takes to get high again. My first experience with drugs was so good that I had to try it again just to make sure that I liked it. I did, but I still hated the comedown. Ecstasy would keep me so wired on the comedown that I couldn't sleep a wink; I would be up all night hoping that another pill would drop out of the sky. I wish I could have foreseen that – opening this door to Satan would cost me years of suffering. But I kept experimenting with drugs, starting a vicious cycle that made me consume more pills every weekend.

At the time, I didn't see anything wrong with it. After all, I still had the power to turn down my roommates when they offered me a line of cocaine. That made me feel proud. I spent about a year continuing this clubbing cycle with my exciting new friends. One month, Renee was short on rent. This wasn't even the first time; we were all short on money (maybe our drug addiction problem was partly to blame?)

Renee got the bright idea to go and strip at a club to make money. The idea appalled me, but Renee being Renee, convinced me to accompany her.

"If you are my friend, you would do this with me," she said.

I really was Renee's friend. She had been there for me all this time we were living together. She was always nice to me. I decided that it was my turn to be Renee's good friend.

I agreed to become a stripper, but only temporarily.

Renee and I entered the club. It was dark and freezing. I had dreaded going, but now that I was here, I was even more fearful. I didn't think I could pull it off. The dancers at the club where we hung out were all beautiful and sexy. Renee asked to see the manager. Men in the club were staring at me. I was still debating about whether to return to the car or not when the waitress pointed to the owner – a white-haired man with a white goatee who wore a white suit.

Oddly enough, his name was Whitey. How convenient!

Renee introduced us with self-assurance. Whitey said he would have to see us in our G-strings before we could be hired. I didn't even own a G-string. In fact, I was wearing granny panties.

My mind was racing. Something inside me was telling me that this wasn't right and that it would only lead to more problems. When I told Whitey that I wasn't wearing a G-string, I had secretly hoped it would blow my chances. But Whitey said it was okay; he just needed a look at my body to see if he liked what he saw. The club (he said) had a high set of standards.

This did not help with the butterflies in my stomach at all.

After Whitey's careful evaluation, I found myself with a new job. Weirdly enough, Renee was turned down because she had tattoos on her legs; it made Renee give me the cold shoulder for a week. After weighing the pros and cons, I finally decided that I could really use the money to pay for my college tuition. I would give it a try. Strip club, here I come!

Reminiscing about my first-time dancing on the stage that first night still scares me. I was so nervous. I wasn't sure if anyone would like me. All I was hoping for was for men to come throwing a whole bunch of money on stage for me. Up on stage, the lights were bright, and I was getting more nervous. Should I move right? Or left? I was not sure I could even remember how to dance, so I just began to move. At least it was a start.

Certain areas of the stage were so brightly lit that one couldn't see the audience. This was a blessing in disguise for me. If the bright lights kept me from finding out what men in the audience really thought of me, then I couldn't be happier!

On the first night, I didn't know what other strippers thought of their audience, but I concentrated mainly on making sure I wouldn't trip onstage. I always wondered what made these guys notice me at the club. For example, if I was walking down a busy street, would I still stand out to these guys? Would they find me equally enticing if they noticed me in the real world?

That first song seemed to last forever, and I just wanted it to end. When I finally got offstage and counted my money, I realized that I had made only a measly, four dollars. All that stress and worry brought me ... *just four dollars*! It made me feel terrible.

A girl named Chocolate saw me crying and approached. In her infinite wisdom, she told me that I needed to do table dances to make real money. Sure enough, when I looked up and wiped my tears, I saw a girl dancing above a man who almost looked in pain. In fact, he was so eager to be close to the dancing girl's body that it almost seemed to hurt him to refrain from doing so.

At this club, men were allowed to touch the women, but they tried to avoid doing it (in their minds at least) so that they weren't cheating on their wives. I seriously wondered how I would be able to deal with this.

Chocolate told me that I had to go and ask the men if they wanted a dance. If they said yes, I would have to charge them no less than twenty dollars a dance.

So, what did I do with Chocolate's advice?

Nothing.

I just sat alone because I was too shy to walk up to some random men and ask them if they wanted me to dance for them for money.

Later that night, two men came up to me and asked me to dance for them.

So, I did, albeit being nervous and scared. On the first night, I made forty-four dollars. That was a little more than I was making waiting tables, but I wanted to quit dancing; everyone else made hundreds of dollars in that one night. And, I could only manage $44.

When I went home, my roommates encouraged me to keep trying. "You can't give up after one week."

So, I continued to go every day for the next couple of weeks that followed and kept coming back home with $40 a night because I was too afraid to ask anyone for a dance. But on Friday, I came home with $100. From Monday through Thursday, I made $40 a night and on Fridays, I made $100.

This went on for a month and then it hit me: maybe if I try a different club, I'd have better luck? I was told about a club named Fantasy where you could dance, and the girls made a lot of money, but the men were not allowed to touch at all.

So, I gave it a shot, and it was a success: more guys asked me to dance, and they paid a lot better. I was making about $200-300 on a slow night and $500-700 on the weekends. For a while, I was the highest-paid girl in the club.

I was happy. I had saved a good amount of money and finally decided to attend San Jacinto College. I eventually joined the college, but the late hours at Fantasy led to poor class attendance and poor grades, so I dropped my courses.

During my time there, I made friends with the head of the psychology department who feared that if I dropped out of college, I may never return.

This was not something I wanted to think about, but it did weigh heavily on my mind.

I continued to dance and make a lot of money in my first year of dancing. Then, one night, I went to another club named the Gold Cup as a favor to a friend. This was a higher-class club. The club was beautiful on the outside. However, no one ever warned me that I could go to jail for doing something that was legal. I danced for an undercover officer and set myself up for real failure – I landed in jail.

I called my mother to let her know that I had gotten arrested because I was afraid that she might end up being the one to take my fingerprints if they transferred me to the county jail. It was better to give the unpleasant news myself.

"Hi, Mom ... I've something to tell you ... I am in jail."

"Why are you in jail?"

"Public lewdness."

"Deanna, I don't believe it."

That comment rang in my ear for a while. I would like to say that I wised up right away after that. The tone of my mother's voice indicated that I had disappointed and even hurt her. I didn't want to hurt her; like most children, I wanted her approval. I had started a lifestyle that I had grown accustomed to; quitting now would render me financially disabled.

Amidst all this dancing away, making money, joining college, leaving college, going to jail and everything else in between – God was always in the back of my mind. I don't mean this in a positive way. He was in my mind entirely for different reasons. I was sure He didn't care much about me anymore because I had turned my back on Him.

I had disobeyed Him; why would He help me now? Even while such thoughts plagued my mind, a little part of me told me a different story. It told me that He is still there, calling out to me even if all my sins had landed me in jail.

Days turned into weeks.

A couple of weeks later, after I got out of jail, my mother called me.

"Hi, I just wanted you to know that I love you, and the Lord has not forgotten about you." Her call warmed my heart and made my eyes well up with tears. After we hung up, I kept replaying the conversation in my mind. Maybe it was a sign that He still loved me?

I wasn't ready yet to leave this life I'd made, but knowing God was still there felt good. I had never really meant much to anyone. I was always second to someone or just not enough. As a dancer, I knew people thought I was attractive and special – even if it was just for one night of lights and music.

4. What You Need to Know about Strippers

First things first, never confuse a stripper with a prostitute. Although it may seem the same, it is not. Girls who are trying to get ahead will dance; girls without any hope will prostitute. Having firsthand experience with being a stripper, I realized there are many things people don't understand about strippers and strip clubs. The people who go to the clubs don't talk about why they go or what happens there, and strippers do not spend a lot of their free time telling people about how they pay their bills.

To understand me and my story though, I should probably explain a few things about strippers, customers, and strip clubs.

Strippers are a strange and rare breed, so much so that it would seem easy to pick them out of a line-up. Most dancers love attention and like being listened to, but they are also very good listeners. They are not always starved for attention. Sometimes the attention can be overwhelming. A dancer who is making money and getting plenty of attention is having both her material and emotional needs being met. This is an ugly cycle though because every dancer has off nights. Nothing is more devastating to a dancing girl's ego than going to work and realizing that no one is interested in her that night ... or even worse, that week. During such times, past feelings of rejection and abandonment will resurface.

For me, dancing gave me a confidence I did not have before.

I was raised in a culturally diverse area, and we were taught to at least outwardly pretend to respect one another, regardless of any differences we may quietly perceive. Most of the people that I had encountered up until this point in my life had acted the same way. My neighborhood was a nicer, suburban one, and I had no problems fitting in. Until I began dancing, I hadn't felt like discrimination was a huge issue for people of my generation and background.

At a strip club, racial issues are out in the open and never brushed aside in the name of "good manners." On some nights, people did not want me to dance for them because I didn't have blonde hair and blue eyes. On other nights people only wanted me because they had some African-American girl fantasy. The strip club is all about fantasies: fulfilling and recreating fantasies of how people think things are and how they wish they could be.

A man who comes into a strip club is looking to have this fantasy fulfilled, to have some perception reinforced, to get the attention he is not getting elsewhere. When a man walks into a club, he can finally get any girl he wants to dance – that is the perception that the dancers give as they vie for customers to pay them for dances. They compete for the men's money, but the men tell themselves that the dancers are competing for them although both sides know it goes no further than a dance and maybe conversation. The only potential downside for a man coming to a strip club is if he doesn't have any money. As they say, "No money, no honey." Even then, the idea of a beautiful woman flirting and acting interested may be enough to bring him satisfaction.

A strip club sells a fantasy, and the men are happy to buy it up. Whether it is the stripper herself or the men on the other side, everyone knows that none of this is real.

What is that one quality that a stripper needs to have a lucrative career? Most would say that she needs amazing dancing skills. And I agree, I mean, if she doesn't know how to dance, what is she really going to do up on stage? Juggle?

I don't think so.

But for a girl seeking to make a living as a stripper, there's something even more important than dancing – awesome acting skills.

In order to fulfill the fantasy, a successful dancer must also be a trained and convincing actress. While new dancers might naïvely believe that dancing is enough to make money, girls who have stayed for longer know that they aren't just paid to dance. Think about all the acting prowess a dancer has to possess just to convince someone to part with $20 for 4 minutes of their time: hopping onto a stranger's lap, pretending that he, the most hideous creature, is handsome – despite his bad breath, receding hairline and big gut, after which they will have to move ten feet away to the next heinous men and do it all over again.

You need pretty good "faking it" skills to do this effectively. It is incredibly difficult pretending to be interested in a man who is anything but appealing to you.

So, I did – I learned the skills and I learned to act pretty well, at least well enough to convince customers in the strip club. I wasn't perfect, and some nights, there just wasn't enough money in the world, so I knocked the heck out of a few of the guys who touched me the wrong way. However, I learned to mask my emotions pretty well overall – not the best skill to have as a woman of faith, as it makes it a lot easier to hide from yourself and your own emotions as well.

I would be lying if I didn't mention that a lot of these dancers have experienced hurt in some way – mentally or physically. It is common for a girl who has been raped, molested or maybe suffered some type of abuse or neglect, to become a dancer. They have already developed some of the masking and hiding skills, and they have dealt with men touching them the wrong way as well. I have known fellow dancers whose mother or father sold their virginity for drugs or money. At the time, I was too self-absorbed to realize it, but it's easier for a dancer to rationalize the poor treatment at the club if all you have ever known is poor treatment.

At least in the club, you are getting paid for it. So, it makes your job of "putting on a show" seem worthwhile.

Being a dancer is about being able to control your environment and men. This is another reason that damaged women work in strip clubs

– it offers a sense of control missing in their day-to-day lives. A strip club is the best place for a woman to try to control a man. In the club, I was able to have a certain amount of control, albeit a false one.

In fact, the male customer likely has a wife at home; almost all of them told me they had wives or were in a committed relationship. The stripper has no control over a man who answers to another woman, even if she is the one sitting on his lap at the moment. He will tell you how great and beautiful his wife is, yet, he is paying to have you do a sensual dance for him.

Men like to believe that no matter what, they've still got it – sex appeal, attractiveness – whatever causes women to chase men. So, they take a chance and gamble with their families and with the relationship with their wives. I guess they feel like they are not really cheating since they are not having sex. Well, I believe (and I think most women would agree) that this is cheating. More importantly, touching a naked woman who is not your wife is worth a death sentence to your marriage. Most men that I meet in strip clubs are incredibly unattractive; I can never take them seriously. Now and then, a nice gentleman would venture into the club. Perhaps we ought to give him the benefit of the doubt? But what kind of man voluntarily steps into a strip club?

Hustler – that is a word that would definitely describe a dancer. While you might find a hustler at any place, you are sure to find a bunch of them at strip clubs. These girls have to be very inventive to convince a man to come up with $20 for a four-minute dance. Strippers would make great stockbrokers, used car salespeople and pharmaceutical salespeople. These women can sell anything! A stripper closes the deal, makes her money and gets the job done – usually in four minutes or lesser.

Dancers are very straightforward; if they are thinking it, then they have already said it. This is the strange nature of strippers: some of the most beautiful women – all in one place and dressed to the T – with the most horrific words spewing out of their lips. On any given night, the words that come out of a stripper's mouth are more shocking than those from a sailor's mouth. Personally speaking, this has also been one of the hardest habits to get rid of, long after I left the strip club and moved into the professional world. My faith, no matter how strong, doesn't make it any easier for me to shut my mouth when I stub my toe!

In addition to saying what you think without running it through your inner censor, there is another unwritten rule of dancing: territory. When a new girl comes in, she better stick to the rules and stay away from the other girls' repeat customers, or she will have a bunch of five-inch heels sticking out of her back. If a regular girl gets into a fight with a new girl, all the girls in the club will jump the new girl, and the new girl never returns. Inside the club, a gang mentality prevails where acts of meanness can seem perfectly normal.

As crazy as the whole world of stripping sounds, there is only one reason why a girl becomes a dancer in the first place: the money. I made a lot of money dancing, and before I got into drugs, I was able to live a great lifestyle on my own income. If a girl can keep her nose clean (literally), she usually can save a lot of money. The problem for me was that I wasn't able to keep my head straight and my nose clean. The things I had to do to make the money, turned me into something so hideous on the inside that I couldn't keep my faith or morals. I lost myself to the sin, the glamour, and the greed.

I traded in my morals for what?

Absolutely nothing.

5. Once Bitten, but Never Shy

After getting arrested, you would think I would have gotten smart enough to see where my life was going and stop dancing, but nope.

I had never been a quitter and was not going to become one now.

Immediately after getting out of jail, I was afraid of being arrested again so I stopped dancing for a while. I couldn't stick to it though and went back soon enough – mainly because of the money.

There weren't jobs out there for a girl like me that paid that well. I had been dancing a year, and although I was using ecstasy on weekends, I didn't do cocaine and didn't want to. I would dance, I told myself, but I would know where to draw the line.

One night there was a phone call in the locker room from someone looking for a dancer to perform at a party for $100. No one else wanted to do it, so I jumped at the opportunity. I told the man on the phone that $100 would only buy 15 minutes of dancing plus tips. We exchanged phone numbers, and I got directions from the man on the phone. I headed out alone, thinking it would be just another frat house party of young boys wanting quick entertainment.

When I got to the house, it was not much nicer than a shack, just a little white house in desperate need of a paint job. It was dark in front of the house, and there weren't any outside lights. I walked up to the house and knocked. From the driveway, I could see parked cars behind the house (which presumably belonged to people at the party).

The man who opened the door was short (about five feet seven inches) with dark, curly hair. He looked like he worked out. He was happy to see me, and he said his name was Jared. But no one else was there. I remember thinking, this doesn't look like much of a party. I could have been working at the club. I needed a new car and wanted to earn enough for a good down payment. I didn't have time to hang around a party which hadn't even begun.

"Is this the house for the party?" I asked Jared. No, It was just him. I should have gotten the clue.

"Come on in. Let me get your money," he said, as I walked into a room which looked like it was decorated in the late 70's. He locked the door after me. The more I looked around, the more I needed this dance to be over.

"It's only a 15-minute dance," I told him.

"That's fine," he said, handing me the money.

"Where is everybody?" I asked again. "I thought this was a party. Do you have any music?" I didn't think to bring a radio.

"The others did not show up," he said. "Go ahead and dance."

"I need music." I was beginning to get weirded out. It was just me and him. I should have walked out. Normally, the girls brought a bodyguard along. But since it was only going to be for 15 minutes, coupled with the fact that it was on such short notice, I had come by myself.

He put out a line of cocaine and asked, "Do you want some?"

"No thanks," I replied. "Let's do the dance now. I have to get back to the club." That wasn't a lie (even though the guy was creeping me out). I still needed to make more money that night.

"Go ahead," he said. I took off my quartz watch and placed it on the table where Jared had sniffed his lick of cocaine. I was always nervous about being around cocaine. I knew it was no good to be around. I slowly danced near him in awkward silence. I took off my clothes until nothing was left except my T-back. I began to dance around him and on him, keeping my eye on the quartz. Time seemed to go by even slower when there was no music. Then, he grabbed me by my arms and pulled me close and, with one of his legs behind mine, forced me on the second couch. He climbed on top of me and forced my legs apart, smiling the whole time.

I managed to kick him off of me. I got up and ran to the door. But it was deadbolted and the key was missing. I stood frozen as I realized that I'd just been locked inside the house. While we struggled, the man's elbow banged against my left temple, disorienting me as the man dragged me by the hair to his yellow paisley couch.

"Stop, get off of me! This is not why I'm here!" I slapped at him and tried to loosen his grip on my hair weave. "Please stop! This is not why I'm here!" I tried digging my feet into the carpet to resist, but it was of no use. Eventually, he got me back to the sofa, this time on my stomach. I could not believe what was happening. I kept fighting, I wasn't going to give in. I was getting raped. In those awful, awful minutes, my mind had gone completely blank. The more I struggled, the more excited he became. Finally, he finished. He turned me around and began licking and kissing my face. I was sick to my stomach.

Jared bent down to do another line of coke. He pulled out a pouch from under the couch. I rose up slowly and walked across the small room to get my top. Jared did not bother to take off my t-back, so I picked up my skirt. I was shaking all over. I could not control it.

"Come back over here and sit," Jared said. "We're not done partying." I felt sick just having to look at him. On my way back to the sofa, I noticed a key on a small coffee table, next to the recliner where I first began dancing. That had to be the key to the front door.

I sat down without being able to put on my shoes. Jared reached under the sofa, pulled out another baggie and threw it at me. I took the pouch and placed it in my top. An hour or two ago at the club, I decided to go to this "party" — thinking that I would be just doing what I do every night: dance for money. And here I was, a *freaking victim*. He raped me and paid me to do it. This had been a setup straight from the beginning. Everyone must have known it but me. There was nothing I could do.

Up to that point, I had never touched cocaine. I had limited myself to ecstasy and Crown Royal because I thought I could control myself that way. But now, everything had changed. My world had been thrown off balance with one bad decision.

I snapped back to reality when Jared told me he had to go to the restroom.

"When I come back, we're going to party again," he said, smiling.

"So, you're going to rape me again." I said, with a combination of disdain and fear. "This ... is this what you call a party?"

Jared laughed, grabbed one of my boobs and licked my neck and ear. I wanted to throw up.

As soon as Jared left. I grabbed my purse and the key, praying that it was the right one. The door opened, and I carefully shut it behind me. I was glad I had left the keys in my car and sped out of the driveway. My heart was pounding so hard. I did not know if I would make it out alive.

I went back to the club where I would be safe. I went to the bathroom to look in the mirror. I wanted to see if Jared had left any marks on the side on my head where he had elbowed me. The area where he hit me was tender to the touch.

Some dancers I knew walked into the bathroom. I pulled the coke out of my top. This was Jared's coke, his "prize" for raping me. Still upset, I offered to share the cocaine with the other girls. The girls were shocked; they knew that I didn't touch the stuff. But after what had just happened, taking cocaine didn't seem particularly awful; I needed to block out what had just happened.

My thoughts were a mess. Was I really raped? Was it just a figment of my imagination? Can a stripper even get raped? Did I deserve this for being so stupid? So many difficult questions raced through my mind, and the only thing which helped to quiet my brain down was drugs. The next day, I felt as if his smell was still on me. It made me nauseous. I hated myself for what I had let happen.

I hated not just that man, but all men. Someone needed to pay.

The next night at work, I began to get phone calls in the locker room. They were all from

Jared. He would even change his name if I ignored him so that I would answer the phone.

Jared was a persistent man. He called me for two weeks straight because I had given him my home phone number. I told him to stop, but the calls just kept coming. I even called the police, but they said they couldn't do anything about him calling. However, they told me to get a Caller ID. I called the phone company, ordered it and blocked his number as well.

When the block took effect, I was relieved, but it only took Jared a week to figure out how I was avoiding him. He started calling from different numbers, but the Caller ID showed that it was a number I didn't know or recognize, so I would not answer the phone. I was annoyed but also incredibly angry. All I could think was, how dare this jerk rape me and still have the nerve to stalk me.

I never reported the rape, because I assumed that no one would believe a stripper turned down sex, especially for money. I felt like my hands (and tongue) were tied.

After a few more weeks, the phone calls stopped, but I began to be followed home by a van. Was there no stopping this man? One afternoon at the club, I received a package: a shoe (one of the pair of shoes I had left at Jared's). I couldn't understand. He already got what he wanted; why wouldn't he leave me alone?

Some days I would see Jared's van, and I asked friends to spend the night with me. Their presence made me feel safe. Eventually, Jared stopped following me in his van, but showed up at the club where I worked.

Unbelievable! My initial reaction was fear; I thought I might pee on myself out of fear and sheer trepidation. I recall the shock that took over Hester when she spotted her long-lost husband in the crowd! But unlike Roger Chillingworth (who sends Hester to America but then abandons her later), Jared had followed me into my club!

But this was my club. I had many people backing me. Having some of the guys at the club beat Jared up scared me a little. What if Jared started to haunt my life in crazier ways?

But I needed some way to show Jared that I wasn't alone. The club owner never let anyone mess with us. After I told my boss what was going on, he and his bouncers took Jared outside and kicked his butt.

In an instant, Jared was no longer a problem for me. But the coke problem was another story. I wish getting rid of that problem would be as easy as getting rid of Jared. I later learned that the second problem wasn't going away anytime soon.

6. Missing All the Turns

I was hooked on cocaine. It helped me cope with all the stress in my life. I knew it was wrong, but it felt so right.

Every time I did cocaine, I fell deeper into the pit. But giving up the habit is not as easy as just putting it away and never looking there.

So, I continued doing cocaine.

If being arrested hadn't been enough to bring me back to God, rape was certainly another opportunity to reassess my life and priorities. And what did I do? Just like I did several times before, I chose to pass up this opportunity of getting my life back together. My mind was split into two; the evil part would tell me to take the leap of faith, leave this life of sex and glamour, give up cocaine and retrace my steps back to God.

But that seemed like so much work!

So, I took the "easier" route and continued dancing despite these clear signs to stop.

Men would often confuse dancers for prostitutes; I never liked that. But it happened so many times that eventually, I came to terms with this too.

I decided that if guys wanted to get screwed, well, I was going to screw them! Sometimes men would proposition me outright for sex. Whenever one of them made it clear he was propositioning me for sex, I would reply that for $300, yes, I would screw him. Not in those exact words, of course; I wasn't a stupid girl. If the man agreed, I would send him into one of the private rooms after collecting my money. Then, I would send my manager in after him. My manager would tell this man that if he didn't leave right away, he would go directly to jail. I never once had any intentions of having sex with these bastards. These men never argued, but just left. My manager would get a hundred dollars, and I would keep the other two. The men had been screwed — not like they wanted — but how I thought they should be. This is what they deserved for mistaking me for a prostitute as that rapist Jared had done. I was never a prostitute and I'd be dammed to allow someone to mistake me for one.

I was making money again. It didn't matter how many guys I "screwed" or how many dances I was performing on a given night, it all ended up going to clubbing and cocaine. Hundreds and hundreds of dollars going right up my Hoover, and I didn't stop to think about what I was doing. Everything I was doing, from misleading customers to using drugs, was morally wrong.

The old Deanna was gone, and in her place, was an angry animal ready to strike out at anyone who tried to get too close.

One night in the club there was another raid. Someone pointed at me and said to go sit by the door. I had just arrived and hadn't done any dancing. Why was I being arrested again? What was going on?

My boss had known me to be a clean dancer, and after my last arrest a year before, I knew better than to dance too close to customers. So why was I being singled out? The officer who arrested me would not say. After I posted bond, I found out it was for solicitation of prostitution. There had to be a mistake. Yes, we ran scams, but only on jerks that solicited me.

I had never or have ever solicited anyone for sex.

At that point in my life, I felt sex was to be given away for free, and boy, did I give it away. I could not believe this was happening. There was no way I was guilty. I was so confused. When I got to court the next week, the district attorney read the report, and I finally knew what had happened. One week before the raid, a girl named Macy (Hollywood) solicited an off-duty officer. They had her name, address and phone number, but because we were both black, they had confused me with her. I was guilty of being black at the wrong time.

When I eventually saw pictures of Hollywood, I couldn't believe that anyone could confuse us. Yes, we both had grey eyes. Yes, we both had long hair, and yes, we were both black. But I was prettier, and Hollywood looked a lot more ghetto.

All I needed to do was show that I was in Austin with friends on the night Hollywood had allegedly solicited the cop. It was not easy. I had to track down a few people by phone and get them to confirm the details. But eventually, I gathered enough evidence and witnesses to leave no doubt that the police had arrested the wrong girl.

For weeks after that, the police knew they had made a mistake. This arrest mix-up was frustrating like nothing else. Why was I held for something I didn't even do?! Again, that other part of my brain started to speak up to me. It told me to focus on what kind of awful mess my current employment had landed me in. It told me to take this as a warning sign and change tracks.

I knew I needed a change in employment, but I still would not cry out to God. Sometimes, even now, I think about how my life would have turned out if I had just pulled the brakes and turned to God for guidance.

Eventually, the charge of prostitution was dismissed, but the arrest remained on my record. This stupid mix up ended up costing me a lot more than just a bruise to my already bruised ego.

For eleven years after that, I could not get a job because prostitution was on my criminal record. All arrests show up on your background checks, even if they are dismissed. Eventually, I was able to get that arrest expunged, but for a long time, the prostitution label closed doors for me. Every time I would try to steer myself on a different career route, the prostitution label would follow me and ruin my chances. Just as the scarlet A on Hester's bosom started to become a permanent part of her identity, I was beginning to think that my past sins would mark me for the rest of my life.

By the way, I later learned that Hollywood – the girl responsible for this wrongful arrest – ended up getting twenty-five years for armed robbery. There is no justice like justice, and eventually even Hollywood had to pay heavily for her sins, but what good did that do to me? As far as I was concerned, the damage had already been done.

I am not trying to downplay my choices or justify them; I knew that the path I was on was less than noble; dancing my nights away in front of random men was hardly something a person aspired to be doing. But if there is one consolation in all this, it is that I was honest with myself.

I was honest with myself that I needed money. I was honest with myself that other than stripping, no other job would put that much money on the table. I was honest with myself that I had no other talents, skills or even the education that's required to hold a respectable career other than stripping. I was honest with myself that I knew God was there for me, but I just did not want to do the hard work of turning my metaphorical car in His direction.

But what good is honesty when it won't save you from trouble?

7. Walking Dead

You don't necessarily have to die to be dead; you could be living and still be dead. Things in my life continued moving in a downward spiral. Whatever money I was making, I was spending to buy drugs. Each time I needed a little more than last time to get high, which meant buying more drugs and spending an increasing amount of money.

So, I kept spending money on drugs, kept on doing them, kept on going to parties. My social life was still not going anywhere though. I met a few interesting men and even dated them for a while, but my partying always got in the way. My heart was broken every time a relationship ended, and nothing could fill the emptiness inside. After the last guy I had dated left town, I decided I could not stand my life anymore – that is, until he decided to come back. As it turned out, he came back to town just to break up with me. Can you imagine my luck?

And what did I do? Did I cry? A little. To ease the pain, I did the only thing I knew best: took cocaine to rush through my days and Xanax to put myself to sleep.

The pain and emptiness would not go away, and I didn't want to try to live anymore. I was dying inside. My life had become just a joke; these were not the plans I had for my life. I used to have dreams and plans, but barely made the rent; drugs and heartbreaks were never part of those plans. I was now 24 and had nothing. Something had to give!

I had already been up for a couple of days on a coke bender, so I was not thinking clearly. That was when he broke up with me. I got a twelve-pack of Budweiser and a whole bunch of pills — 50 to be exact. I filled my bathtub with water and got in. I drank every beer and took all the pills. I began to cry.

"God," I thought to myself. "I know my life has been a bunch of crap and it's a big joke, but I can't do this anymore. I hurt all the time, and I have no reason to live." I felt my consciousness leaving, and I managed one more thought. "If you can't give me a reason to live and if there is no reason for me to live, please ... just ... let ... me ... die." I remember asking forgiveness for everything I had been doing and for turning my back on him.

The people that I was partying with found me in the tub after a couple of hours. I was unconscious. It is always a bad situation when someone OD's; often the person will get left behind in a trash can or dumpster somewhere. Since I was already at my place, my friends decided to wait it out. They wanted to see if I would pull through. One girl called poison control, and they told her to get me to throw up and to call an ambulance. They also told her that I would need to go to the hospital no matter what because the number of pills I had taken would cause inevitable liver damage.

There were too many drugs around for them to call an ambulance, though, so they decided to make me throw up and hope for the best. When I finally woke up, I went into my living room naked and told them to keep it down, that I was trying to sleep. From what I understand, I was unconscious for about forty-eight hours before making that announcement. Everyone in my apartment fell silent for a moment and then began to cheer. I guess no one really wanted to leave me for dead.

Things were slow after my unsuccessful attempt at killing myself. A week later, I didn't feel much better about my life. I still felt like there was no reason for me to live. I noticed that I was getting really sick all the time and super hungry.

This was particularly strange because usually when you use cocaine, you don't get hungry.

What was up with that? I backtracked a little and noticed that I hadn't had my period. Could I be pregnant? I know that a lot of women in my shoes would probably think getting knocked up would be like the last thing they would want to deal with, but the very idea of having a baby excited me.

I took a pregnancy test, but it turned out negative. I was back to where I started: down in the dumps. Now, I was even more depressed; at least a baby would have given me a reason to live.

I realized that staying at home all dull and gloomy wouldn't do me any favors. So, I returned to work. I needed to keep busy and earn some money.

One night after work, a co-worker wanted me to come hang out with one of their friends, a guy, of course. His name was Trent, and little did I know how important of a part in my life he would play over the following months.

Trent had a beautiful home in La Porte. He seemed to be doing really well for himself, but he had a pretty big cocaine problem ... even bigger than mine. Trent's problem had been there for a while, and I didn't know it. I was so smitten by Trent's big home that his cocaine problem was the last thing on my mind. After all, I had the same problem; what right did I have to judge?

I started hanging out with Trent a lot. It was only a matter of time till things got physical. Trent and I kept seeing each other and grew closer even though both our lives were a mess. During the four months we were together, Trent lost his home and truck and destroyed his credit. I lost my apartment and car; we were homeless. We had both made money, but we lost everything.

I did notice one strange problem though; whenever I would try to do any cocaine I would get sick and immediately throw up. I had also put on weight.

Could I be pregnant? I did not want to get my hopes up like last time. I decided to go to the Crisis Pregnancy Center near Pasadena and get myself tested.

The test showed that I had been pregnant for a couple of months. I couldn't believe it! Did this mean that when I tried to kill myself a couple of months back, I was already pregnant? But why did the test show negative then? My mind was a blur, partly from confusion and partly from excitement.

The people at the Crisis Pregnancy Center were very nice. They gave me a lot of pamphlets and information on how to earn things I needed for the baby, like a bassinet.

There was no question that Trent was the father. He himself had taken me to the crisis center, but he wasn't at all happy that I was pregnant. Did that matter to me? Not in the least! I was pregnant, I was finally going to have a baby of my own. At this point in my life, this was the most important thing that had ever happened. Whenever I brought up my pregnancy, he would get quiet and somewhat frustrated. While that was annoying, I thought I could just ignore and avoid it by not bringing up my pregnancy – until he demanded that I get an abortion.

Trent had his reasons. He was divorced, and he already had one child he didn't see because of his drug use. He was way behind on child support and had no desire to deal with another child when he couldn't even deal with his own.

The baby was a gift, the gift of a new start. God had given me a reason to live. More than anything, I wanted this child, and I wanted to be a good mother. I was hooked on cocaine, but it was making me sick because I was pregnant. I knew I would have to do something drastic, something I didn't want to do but something I knew I had to do for the sake of this child. I had to call my mother!

When I called my mother, she was excited to hear I was happy. I asked if I could come home, and she said "Sure." She told me not to worry about getting a job for at least two months after I had the baby. She was very supportive. I wish I could say all my problems were solved when I turned to my mother, but nothing in life is that simple. I knew a cocaine problem was bad; what I didn't know was that getting over a cocaine problem would be even worse. By going home, I managed to isolate myself from everything and everyone associated with drugs, but that thing still called to me.

In my dreams and when I was awake, I would smell it. This is typical for someone trying to get free of drugs. Sometimes, it's not because they don't want to quit; it is because they mentally can't. The drug dreams are so vivid, and nearly everyone who comes off drugs has them. Every day for the rest of my pregnancy, I craved the stuff. It was complete, unadulterated torment. It was ok though because I knew I was safe at my mother's house and so was my baby. I was really worried about the damage that I may have already done to my baby, so I was very open and honest with the doctors about my drug use and suicide attempt. They ran a lot of tests and found that my baby was going to be healthy, but with any speed drugs, you run the risk of having a hyperactive child. I stayed clean throughout the rest of my pregnancy and looked forward to the time after my son's birth when I could return to drugs. They called to me and I wanted to answer.

8. The Baby Blues: What It is Really Like Being Pregnant

On November 22, 1997, when I was 24, the Lord gave me the most beautiful baby the world had ever seen. At that moment in my life, that beautiful baby boy was a sign that God had been with me through all of the pain and struggles. He seemed so happy. He would even smile. The nurse said it was just gas, but I took it as an angel smiling at me.

As happy as I was to have him, I was still drawn to the club life. Two weeks after his birth I was back at the club dancing. I had to make money for my baby! That's what I told myself, and that is what I told my mother. But dancing was just an excuse to get close to drugs again. My mother was not happy, so she worked out a deal with my aunt in Houston to keep the baby while I worked. Despite her disappointment, my mother tried not to judge me. She would have kept my sweet boy herself, but she worked full time to support her own children (who were still in school).

My aunt was very good to my son, and both he and I were lucky to have her. He lived in her home with her, and I would stop in once a week to bring her a couple hundred dollars or so. I really missed my baby, but I did not want to give up my lifestyle. I continued to dance and live with whomever I wanted. I really didn't have one place to live. My life was still in shambles. I didn't have an education; any other jobs I was qualified for would not even pay for a place to live. I knew I wanted my son back, and I wanted to raise him and be a good mother. I just didn't have any parenting skills.

In an effort to better my life for my baby, I took a job as a waitress at another strip club. This was a step up from dancing, just a little more respectable, but I was still doing drugs. I wanted to quit, but this lifestyle was intoxicating. The lights and the attention drew me in.

After my son was three months old, I decided to get my baby from my aunt. I missed him so much; he was always in my thoughts. He was so innocent and perfect. Every feeling he had toward me was innocent and honest.

I just couldn't bear the distance between us two any longer. I put my foot down and brought my angel back to where he belonged: in my arms. I had found a sitter who would keep him for about two dollars and fifty cents an hour. I knew this girl for more than a year (she had just gotten out of rehab). I decided to trust her; I didn't have any other options. I went to work and was having a pretty good night when the manager told me that I had a phone call in the office. I couldn't imagine who would be calling me at my job this late.

"This is Deanna."

"Ms. Deanna, this is Child Protective Services. We have your son. Is there anyone you can call so that we can release him?"

I felt as if someone had tipped my world over. In that split second every terrible scenario ran through my mind.

"What is this about? Why do you have my son?"

"We need you to come to 6300 Chimney Rock. Are you able to get here?"

I didn't have a car anymore, but I found someone to take me. We drove from Galveston to Houston. It only took us 45 minutes to get there, but it felt like an eternity. I was very fearful of what might have happened and prayed frantically that he was not hurt.

I ran into the CPS building. My mother and little sister were already there with my son. Cameron looked fine, but the glares from my mother and sister told me that everything was far from fine. When I asked what was going on, the attendant said that the police had just brought in the baby, but the report wasn't in yet. He added that my son could not be released to me; if I went anywhere near him, he could be taken from my mother as well.

I still didn't have a clue what was going on or what I had done. I felt my world crashing in on me again. After meeting with the CPS caseworker, I realized that my friend from rehab was far from ready for real-world responsibilities. She had taken my son to a bar, told some strangers to watch him and never returned. The strangers eventually called the police. I had so much rage against that girl Rachel, but I did not acknowledge my own role in this situation. At that time, I was unable to see where I had gone wrong.

At first, the CPS worker doubted my version of events because of my criminal record. My arrests for public lewdness and prostitution caused the CPS worker to judge me very harshly. I tried to explain that the prostitution case was dropped because I was innocent, but it didn't matter. I felt like everyone was against me, even my mother. My son was taken from me, and I couldn't see that I was to blame. That's another thing about drugs – they warp your perception about the people and situations around you. I honestly thought everyone was out to get me, even when they were looking out for my precious son. I was so wrong, but I could only see my side of the situation.

I still could not see how many of my choices were affecting my future; my son had been taken from me, and I could not see my part in the whole thing. Depression set in again; this time I would make Galveston Bay my graveyard. I filled myself with pills and alcohol and walked out into the ocean, the whole time talking to God. I don't remember what I said to Him at that time. But He must have been listening because a man pulled me back to shore and wouldn't leave me until I had gotten home safely. The Lord spared my life for the second time when I didn't deserve it.

I grieved greatly for my son, but I just could not get it right. I needed my pain to end. I barely had a place to live. My grief over the situation was becoming more than I could handle. I had lost my son, and now I couldn't even kill myself right. Why couldn't I just die? I needed an intervention and got one when I got sick. I was pregnant! How could this happen again?

I was very happy with my first child, but this time, I was not sure what to do. I'd lost my first child, and I had just gotten locked out of my friend's apartment for not paying the rent. We had spent all the rent money on drugs; my life was in crisis mode and another child did not seem like the answer. My first baby was only six months old, and now, I was having another one. I was overwhelmed. There was only one solution.

"I have to get rid of this baby."

I would have to come up with some money, and quick. I called John. He was a good guy. He had two obsessions: bodybuilding and his collection of illegal guns! He was very well off too. Despite having all the money and opportunities, John stayed away from drugs. I was actually jealous of that! I met him at the club where he hung out a couple of times.

What I liked about him is that he never judged me. He was always trying to help me by giving me a place to stay or advice about jobs. John liked the idea of my son being around, but I was not ready for someone who didn't do drugs and who worked during the daylight hours.

When I found out that I was pregnant, I turned to him for advice. His answer to my problem was marriage. I didn't want to get married; I also knew that John was possibly not the father. I couldn't lie to him because there was so much caring in his eyes. We strippers have two other cardinal rules: "Never screw over good people," and "Only play players." John was not a player, and I wasn't going to pretend that I loved him; he deserved better than that.

He was actually a good guy, but who wants a good guy when you can have a whole lot of crappy men? That is one of the main issues with wounded women, and I was certainly a wounded woman. I was so busy trying to get love from men who can't or won't love me back that I didn't make time for a man who actually did love me. When a good man actually wants a wounded woman, she runs away to another loser instead. Marriage and this new baby were not in my plans at all. John was completely against me having an abortion, but it was the only thing I could do. I didn't have any other choice. I didn't have a place to live. I couldn't go near my son. I felt I had no one.

A couple of weeks later, after having no more money for a room at the Motel 6, I went to John. I knew he would at least give me some shelter, so I hitched a ride to his neighborhood. Tasha, a girl from the strip club, answered the door. It turns out that Tasha had been helping John to get over me. John had moved on. Tasha made it clear that no other women would be staying in John's home while she was there. That was fair. I had my chance earlier and let it pass me by. It was my loss. That night, I wandered the streets because I had nowhere to go. Nowhere to sleep, nowhere to go, no one to want me.

The next day, I called someone I regarded as an abusive loser. I normally wouldn't seek help from a man like this, but I was desperate.

To my astonishment and relief, this man was willing to help.

"Just find a place and see how much it is," he said, "and I will give you the money."

I got a room at the Motel 6 in Webster. It would be a couple weeks before he would get paid again, so I hitched a ride to Galveston for the next couple of weeks to keep my hotel room. Finally, he called to give some money, and I quoted him a price I thought it would be.

At least I had a roof over my head for now.

9. Next Stop: Wichita Falls

"Loving Christian Maternity Home. This is Barbara."

"Is this the doctor's office?" I asked as I looked down at the fat yellow book I was holding.

"No, this is a maternity home."

"Hmm."

"May I ask what you are looking for?" Barbara asked.

"Well, I thought I was calling an abortion clinic." I was still staring at the book.

The voice on the other side of the phone was so calming; she didn't even sound judgmental.

"Ma'am, I'm not trying to be nosey, but is it for you?" she asked.

"Yes, ma'am."

"Have you thought about maybe adoption? There are a lot of families who would love to have a child."

"Ma'am I don't even have a place to live. If I was to carry a child full term, I don't know if I could just give it away."

"Well, here at Loving Christian, it is always the mother's choice whether or not she wants to keep her baby."

"Really?"

"Really." For some reason, I trusted her, and I didn't even know her.

We began to talk; I told her a little more about me, and she told me about the home, and that they had a bed open. She also told me that they were in Wichita Falls, Texas. Even if I were interested, how in the world would I get there? Wichita Falls was nine hours away.

After I hung up with Barbara, I realized that in the yellow pages I had been looking through the "abortion alternatives" section, not the "abortion" section. I thought a little more about adoption and that maybe it might be a good idea. However, there was still the issue of distance – how would I get to Loving Christian Maternity Home? Maybe there would be a place like Loving Christian Maternity Home closer to Houston, so I got a ride to the Crisis Pregnancy Center in Pasadena and talked to a counselor. This way, I thought, I would have a place to live and not be forced to use drugs anymore. The maternity home needed proof that I was pregnant, and the Crisis Pregnancy Center gave me a letter of proof.

Peggy, the counselor at the Crisis Pregnancy Center, was very helpful. I saw compassion in her eyes as I explained my situation. All the maternity homes in our area accepted only teenagers or mothers who would place their baby for adoption. While I needed a clean place to stay, I wanted to have the choice to keep my baby. Peggy convinced me to call my mother. My mother was happy to hear from me and to know I was okay. She assured me that I could come visit my firstborn and that her intention was never to keep Cameron from me. She also told me that CPS had finally made a decision about my case. If I took parenting classes, I could have my son back. That was great news, but I knew that I still wasn't ready to take care of Cameron.

After several more telephone calls, it was decided that Peggy would drive me the nine hours to Wichita Falls. What an incredible woman! I was struck by the strong faith and commitment that inspired her to drive nine hours for a drug addict she didn't know. Peggy's presence in my life at that point was another sign that God's hand was always at work.

The entire trip, I imagined how my life would be different. I thought about how I could make my mother proud. I would get my son back and go to college. These are the things I wanted; I wanted things to become normal again. I wanted my son to be happy and the new baby to have a good life even if I couldn't be in it. This seemed perfect, I thought. I would be forced to stay away from drugs and my life would have to change for the better.

Norma, the housemother, was there to greet us when we arrived. She had a sweet, calming disposition, but if she had known the real me and what I had been through, I doubted she would even like me. Although I didn't mind people knowing that I had been a dancer, I thought it best to keep my drug history to myself. It was hard to be completely open even with these people.

The house was so peaceful. It was also huge! There was enough space to have a pool built on the roof. My room was big and decorated in a yellow, floral pattern. I had a joint bathroom with the girl in the next room. Maybe I could have a fresh start; it was so calm here that I felt like I could really be a new person.

There was no comparison between what I had in Wichita Falls and what I had in my old place. It was warm and welcoming. In *The Scarlet Letter*, Hester wonders at one point if there existed a place totally different from Massachusetts Bay Colony where she could live without being judged harshly and severely.

For me, that place was Wichita Falls.

Four pregnant girls stayed together in the house. First, there was Candy, the fourteen-year-old who cried rape when her parents found out the guy who got her pregnant was black. Candy felt really bad about crying rape; she knew it wasn't right. She just didn't want to lose her innocence in front of her parents. I didn't judge her. I had made my own mistakes.

Then there was 17-year-old Jenny, who had gotten pregnant by a black boy she actually was in love with. Her parents put her in the maternity home hoping she would choose to place the child up for adoption. Her parents were humiliated and angry. Jenny was strong-willed even though her father refused to talk to her.

The last woman in the house was Erika. Erika was the oldest. She was twenty-eight with long red hair. Erika was on probation for stealing sunglasses from the mall. She and her boyfriend stole things to support their crack habit and eventually got caught.

These three girls and I became like sisters. We all had chores to do, and while I hated chores, I did mine well. Norma and I became close; she treated me like a daughter. This was the first time that I felt like a favorite. That woman had love for me, and I could tell. I was never the favorite growing up, and although I felt special being chosen to work at Ms. Rachel's house, I knew I was never her favorite. Being Norma's favorite made me feel important, like I mattered. I thought that maybe, just maybe, if I mattered to her, then I mattered to God. I had faith when I was younger and genuinely thought I mattered to Him. Later, after all I had been through and everything I had done, I lost that belief. I thought there was no way He could love me or want me in His kingdom. Norma was helping me rebuild that faith and confidence.

Life wasn't always perfect. After about two weeks, I started to go through withdrawals because I had stopped using cocaine. Because I didn't want anyone to know I had used in the first place, I couldn't tell anyone about the physical and mental pain of narcotics withdrawal. It was terrible. It would have helped just to be able to talk about it. I just wanted someone to hold me, so I would wrap my arms around the baby inside me and let her know I loved her and wanted her to be okay. I knew she was a girl because I had just gone to the doctor to get an ultrasound; he confirmed that she was an active and healthy little girl. In addition to suffering from the withdrawals, I was scared about having another baby without having a way to support them.

Months went by, and I really began to miss my son. I wanted him with me. As the baby grew inside me and moved around, it reminded me of when I was pregnant with Cameron. I shared my sadness with Norma, and she offered to let my son come live in the home with us. I was overjoyed; I had not seen him for six months, and he would soon be one year old. His new sister would arrive just a month after his birthday, and I wanted us all to be together.

As I waited for arrangements for Cameron to come live with me, I applied to the housing assistance program through the city. A month later, I was also approved for childcare assistance, so I would have somewhere to put Cameron when he came. At last, my life was finally starting to come together. God was in my life, but Satan wasn't going to make it easy for Him or for me.

I spent a lot of time around Erika, the shoplifter with the crack habit. We confided in each other, but she couldn't wait to get back to smokin' and that was all she talked about. I was focused on staying clean. I was already battling drug dreams and had struggled through the painful withdrawals. Luckily for me, cocaine withdrawals don't kill a person. The physical aches and illness weren't fun, but the mental torment is by far the worst part. Cocaine affects the brain, and I had to battle against Erika's praise for drugs as well as my own strong desires to go back to cocaine. I came here to change my life, to get a fresh start for me and my children. But all Erika talked about was crack. Crack, crack, and more crack.

She wasn't helping!

The first eighteen months are critical when trying to get over any cocaine addiction. If you are lucky, eighteen months is enough for one's brain to go back to normal; some people take longer, and some people are never right again. Cocaine, like heroin, is bad juju.

My mom drove my son up to Wichita Falls one month before I had my little girl. I was so happy to see him and be totally clean when I looked my mother straight in the eye. I did notice, however, that Cameron was very active. He was always happy and always moving. I didn't give much thought to it. I was happy. I had two beautiful children. Now how was I going to support them?

In December, I had Cindy. She was so precious at 7 pounds 11 ounces. It was a tough delivery; we both caught the fever and had to stay in the hospital for several more days. Norma was nice enough to stay in delivery with me, but I was sad to be having a baby with no family around. She was like family, but I still felt alone – it was my second time having a baby without a father, and that's a lonely thing.

After I had Cindy, I went back to the maternity home for a couple more weeks while my body healed from the difficult delivery. In January, when I was healthy again, I moved my children and myself into our new apartment in Wichita Falls. Things seemed to be going my way, and it continued like that – for about six months.

I really enjoyed living in Wichita Falls. During August, the whole town is pumped up because the Dallas Cowboys have their training camp there, and everyone is hoping to see one of the players. While the Cowboys were in town that year, I was working at a new seafood restaurant where I had my very own Cowboy sighting – one of the top Cowboy guys and his son came to the restaurant and invited me to hang out with them at the local bar. Of course, I went, and of course, I got drunk on their tab. Not surprisingly, there was a pretty, dark-skinned girl dancing on the bar by the end of the night. I couldn't help it; they were cheering for me, and you know I love attention!

That wasn't the only run-in I had with a Cowboy. I also got to wait on Troy Aikman and his beautiful blonde fiancée. They were so polite. After giving me a 30% tip, the quarterback told the manager on the way out that he'd received some of the best service he'd had in a long time. Aikman was a very nice guy, and people like him made Wichita seem like such a great place.

I was doing well, paying my bills on time and staying clean. Then, I decided to start hanging out again with Erika – the crack addict from the maternity home. We were both young mothers without a lot of girlfriends, and I didn't think hanging out a bit with Erika would weaken my desire to stay clean. I was wrong and soon, I found myself back on crack.

After about four months of using, something strange happened. I heard my spirit telling me it was time to make a choice – a voice inside me was telling me that this lifestyle couldn't go on. I could either continue to do drugs or choose God. I wasn't sure what to think. Was God really reaching out to me? Or was lack of sleep making me crazy? I knew that this had to be God telling me that it was time to get it together. So, I made my choice. I made a choice to live my life fully rather than die on the streets. I made a choice to be an example to my children. I made a choice to have food in my refrigerator and my electric bill paid on time. I made a choice not to have men running in and out of my home. I made a choice to call my mother and tell her everything that I had been doing.

For the first time, I was even honest with her about the cocaine. I was really and truly ready to be DONE. My mom said she could tell something was going on when I didn't come home for Christmas. She admitted that I had been on her heart, she just never thought it would have been drugs. Her voice sounded disappointed and scared for me at the same time.

I wanted my mother to forgive me just like Hester wanted Dimmesdale to forgive her. When he finds the truth about Chillingworth's reality, he feels betrayed by Hester. Still, he finds in his heart to forgive her and leave justice to God.

My mother did something similar too. She forgave me, but unlike Dimmesdale, my mother was no hypocrite. In this time of need and desperation, she did not abandon me. She got in touch with people at the church she attended. They made arrangements for me to come home with Cameron and Cindy. This was it. I left everything I owned at that point in Wichita Falls and decided to make a clean break.

Things are always easier said than done. I had decided that there was no room for drugs in my life, but the temptation was still there. However, this time, whenever the temptation overcame me, I forced myself to think about what was really important: The Lord and my family.

There were some withdrawals, but not nearly as bad as they had been before. It was like the Lord just took the craving away.

10. The Call

The problem with using cocaine is that you become known as a "person who uses cocaine." Others assume things about people who used to be hooked on cocaine, and all kinds of red flags go up. Employers don't want to give former cocaine users the benefit of the doubt, and this was becoming a big problem for me as I looked for jobs. I spent a lot of time job hunting, and I failed over and over. None of the jobs that would consider hiring me paid enough for both childcare and a roof over my head. Dancing wasn't an option since I had decided to live a clean and righteous life; I had two children now and needed a way to raise them properly.

When the Lord asked me to make a choice in 2000, I committed to my choice and knew my life could never be the same. But, being rejected time and again for jobs, I slipped. In a state of depression, I decided to have a beer at my mother's house; she caught me and was not happy. She forced me to move out within the month. I didn't know what to do. I didn't have a whole lot of options, so I took a job at a McDonald's as a shift manager even though they wanted me to work crazy hours and the grease wreaked havoc on my skin. I had told myself that I would never take a job in a fast food restaurant, but I did what I had to do to make life work for myself and my little ones. I did not last very long because the hours were wearing me out, and the work was physically demanding. Never underestimate fast food workers – it's a tough job!

One morning, after working the graveyard shift at the new 24-hour McDonald's in Bacliff, I awoke to my two children pouring syrup all over me. Another time while I was asleep, my kids had cut my hair. They were always right next to each other when they were doing something devious, like the time they locked me out of the house, so they could rummage through the groceries that I had brought in. They were adorable deplorables, even when they were misbehaving. The syrup and the hair cutting, however, were signs to me: I couldn't keep working at McDonald's.

Life was such a struggle. But, killing myself was no longer an option; I had something to live for – *my children*.

The worst part of being poor is the welfare system. Having to beg for food, standing in those lines, and people treating you like a second-class citizen are experiences I wouldn't wish on my worst enemy. I hated those offices and felt humiliated every time I left. I didn't have any other option. My children needed to eat, and we needed a place to live. A mother sacrifices for her children, even if she has to sacrifice her pride every now and again.

One day, my mother allowed me to use her car to go job hunting, so I was riding around and putting in applications. I decided to sing and pray as I drove around Webster. I turned off the radio so that I could speak to the Lord so He could hear me loud and clear. I began to pray for guidance, and as I prayed harder, I felt like I heard an astral voice emanating from heaven. A voice that could have only been from heaven said, "GO to School." Had I just heard the voice of my Lord? I wanted to go to school. Not to technical school or beauty school, but college. This wasn't just a passing idea, I knew it was God answering my prayer for guidance. The presence in the car was overpowering. I had to obey.

I obeyed immediately. I got off the freeway and headed down to Alvin, Texas. I knew that there was a college there. I drove to Alvin Community College with the knowledge that I was on the right path.

This reminds me of something I heard a preacher say one day. He said, "Do you know how I know the Lord is talking to me? Well, he sounds a lot like me. Do you know what the devil sounds like when he is talking to me? Well, he sounds a lot like me too."

That day the Lord spoke to me, he did sound a lot like me. How could I be confident, then, that it was the Lord guiding me and not just another idea of my own?

Faith.

I had faith that the Lord Almighty was speaking to me. Faith is an essential part of following the right path. To know and understand that God has a strategic plan vital to my spiritual growth.

In Jeremiah 1:5, God tells Jeremiah, "Before you were in the womb I knew and set you apart." If God knew us before we were in the womb and had already set us apart, that means there was already a plan set in motion for our lives. I happen to believe in predestination, and I believe that I have fallen short many times, but if we repent, and we are still alive, there is another strategic plan that is set in motion. The main objective for humans is to stay on course, which we can do by prayer and doing what you know to be right by God. It is not always popular to do the right thing, but it is necessary, and it will lead you to the destination God has waiting for you.

When I arrived at Alvin Community College, I asked someone where I could find the office. The people on the campus were so nice. I walked down a busy hallway, nervous whether I really heard God on the whole go-to-school thing. I was hoping for a sign to confirm that this was what God wanted for me.

I finally made it to where I was supposed to go, and there, they told me to wait for a counselor. When my turn with a counselor came, she was a blond woman in her late forties. In her office, she was playing KSBJ, one of Houston's local Christian radio stations. I took this as the sign I had asked for and felt comfortable telling her that I thought the Lord was telling me to go to school. I was completely honest, telling her, "I don't even have money, but I knew I was to come out here."

"Well, have you thought about what type of degree you would like to get?" she asked.

"Well, I think I would be good at counseling." I never thought I was smart enough for school; I was held back twice in elementary school! I wasn't smart and did not know if I had what it took to be successful at school. I had to believe that if the Lord was leading me in this direction, He had to have a plan for me and my family.

"Wow," she said. "It just so happens that the mental health department has scholarships for people who want to become a licensed chemical dependency counselor or an LCDC. These people get their associate's degree in mental health and get licensed as an LCDC. And if you wanted, they could transfer you to the University of Houston to get your bachelor's degree in psychology or something behavioral." I had asked for a sign, but this was more like a billboard. Was God really going to give me a scholarship to college? My counselor sent me over to speak to Dr. J. Carrier, head of the mental health department.

Dr. Carrier was a well-educated man with red hair and glasses which hung from the bottom of his nose. His attitude made the interview easy and pleasant. He never made me feel like I was less than him or beneath him because I was less educated. He was so approachable!

He informed me that the scholarships would cover all of my classes as well as books. I could not believe how quickly all this was happening. I barely made it through high school; how was I going to make it through college? College was for the big boys. I was in my very late twenties with two children, and I really didn't have a place to live. I went ahead and filled out all the paperwork. Just like that, I was officially registered for college; classes would begin in two weeks.

When I got back to my mother's house, she was not happy that I had been gone so long with her vehicle; she wasn't sure what might have happened. And with all that had happened to me, I didn't blame her for thinking that way!

I was excited about starting school again. Even though I was tempted to tell my mother about it, I didn't because I wasn't sure how or even if it would work out.

I put all this aside to focus on more pressing matters. Because the last time I thumbed through the Yellow Pages brought such a positive result, I tried my luck again, looking for available shelters. Many of them required clients to leave the shelter during the day to seek work. That wouldn't work out for me because of my children and lack of childcare. Another obstacle I hadn't even considered – childcare! How was I going to go to school if I didn't have anyone to look after my kids?

Dread crept up my spine. Was the Lord setting me up just to be disappointed? He gave free tuition, and I wouldn't be able to use it. Maybe He didn't tell me to go after all ...

What horrible luck. I even got upset with myself for not even having thought about childcare before I registered for the classes.

The next day, I borrowed my mother's car again, giving her a set time when I would return. I drove back to Alvin Community College to unregister for my classes, crying all the way.

I asked over and over again, "Why, Lord?" My faith was wavering. Although I truly believed that I had heard from God, why was it so difficult to make this work?

I checked in to see the counselor I had talked to before; tearfully, I told her how I would have to be a college dropout before I had even started because I had no childcare.

The woman calmly listened as I explained my difficulties. "Let's see what we can do," she said.

She brought me to another office where I met another counselor who introduced herself as the childcare facilitator for the college. She told me that they had a certain number of childcare scholarships, but unfortunately, they had allocated all of them already.

"Thank you for your help," I told her as I turned to leave, heartbroken.

"Wait a minute," she said. "I have a friend that works for the Texas Work Source. I'm going to call her. Hold on a minute."

My pulse quickened.

After the childcare facilitator talked on the phone to her friend, she handed me a business card. "I'm not making any promises," she said, "but my friend might be able to help."

An hour later, I arrived at a big brown shiny building for Texas Work Source, hoping to get an appointment (though I was prepared for disappointment). I asked to see the name of the woman on the business card. Minutes later, an attractive woman with brown shoulder-length hair approached me. "You must be the young lady from Alvin Community College. Tell me how I can help you."

Wow, I wouldn't need an appointment. Maybe God was working for me after all!

Nervous about meeting this woman, I decided to be completely honest. I explained how God delivered me from drugs, then told me to go to school and how I could get a scholarship, but, I might have to drop out before I started because I couldn't afford daycare. Did I just really tell this woman God spoke to me. I felt sure that she would have me escorted out.

The Work Source Regional Superintendent, the man in charge, was there that day and overheard everything as my story tumbled out. He stepped into the conversation and said,

"So, God told you to go to school, huh?" He stared me right in the eye. He wanted to see if I was lying or just crazy.

"Umm, yes, sir." In my heart, I knew the Lord had been talking to me in the car a few days ago. I wouldn't back away from that statement – even if the Superintendent thought I was crazy.

"I haven't met many young women like you," the superintendent said. "As a matter of fact, if you want to go to school, we will pay for your childcare and schooling."

"Well, sir, ACC has said they were paying for my schooling and books."

"Ma'am, I am never in one of these offices, and the paperwork I am doing for you today would normally take a couple of months to get to me.

In most cases, it means that the person applying will be put on a waiting list. But I'll see to it that the paperwork gets done immediately so this won't happen. We want to pay for your school, books, and childcare." As the man began doing my paperwork, I kept my mouth shut like a smart girl. I didn't want to do anything to jinx this miraculous offer.

I could not believe it; was my luck finally starting to turn around? Two places wanted to give me money for school!

The man gave me a card and said they might be able to help with gas. Then he vanished. If I hadn't had the papers, contracts, codes of ethics and so many other things to sign, I might have thought I had imagined him. If you think my mind was blown at this point, you have no idea. Just wait!

I looked at the card that the Superintendent had given me. It was for the Texas disability office and it was right around the corner. Apparently, recovering from drugs was considered a kind of short-term disability. When I arrived there, I met a lady named Siad; she was a beautiful woman in a wheelchair. I walked in with a card and walked out with another organization that wanted to pay for my school and books; they even gave me twenty dollars a week in gas money (which at the time was more than adequate).

God had organizations fighting to pay for my college. I think that is called confirmation.

11. Back to School, Back to Life

The Lord made it possible for me to go to school; doing the actual schoolwork was a totally different matter. Unfortunately, I had never been a good student, and I always struggled with studying. I had even been held back in first and third grade, so you could imagine how anxious and unsure of myself I felt when starting college. If I had problems in third grade, how in the world would I survive college?

My kindergarten teacher was tall, blonde and beautiful, and she had one of the nicest smiles. Because of the number of students in the class, I don't remember the teacher ever having time to talk to me. I vividly remember one day when the teacher walked around the classroom, praising their drawings.

After the teacher said to the student next to me how nice her picture was, I wanted the teacher to say she liked my picture too. So, I drew a picture just like the one the girl next to me had drawn: a girl in a dress with C-shaped hair that was colored black. I felt sure that this drawing would earn me a compliment from the teacher.

I raised my hand excitedly to get the teacher's attention.

"Is my picture pretty?" I asked.

"No, it's ugly!" she said, scrunching her face up and glaring at me as she continued walking around the classroom, monitoring the progress of her students.

I was crushed. It is ridiculous that one comment said to me so long ago still had so much power over me. I believed I was not smart enough, I wasn't good enough, and I could not do the work, so I didn't. Never good enough.

And now, here I was ... about to go back to college. When classes were about to start, there was much anticipation about what it might be like. Are my teachers going to like me? How long before I fail? Are there going to be any cute guys? (Well, I was still me!)

When I played volleyball and basketball in junior high school, I was often ineligible due to grades. In the eighth grade, I realized it was no longer popular to be stupid, and I wanted to fit in with students who were going somewhere. It was not easy, and all I could muster up with my study habits were high C's, but this was better than I had ever done. Really, I asked myself as I prepared to start my classes at ACC, how are you going to make it through college? College would be a whole different ballgame.

In all this anticipation, my first day of class arrived. You would not believe what the class was about: drug use and abuse!

God sure has a good sense of humor.

This class was always interesting; it covered many drugs and the effects they had on the body. Sometimes, I felt like I had already tried every drug in the book, but apparently (and fortunately!) that was not true. I never realized the myriad of substances people could abuse. I never truly understood their effects on the body and brain until taking that class.

My fascination with the subject matter paid off. At the end of that first semester, I had A's and B's! Teachers talk about "rigor and relevance"; well, studying about drugs as a disease was already relevant to my life. If a student believes that a subject is relevant, they are more likely to remember and retain the facts and concepts.

If the Lord tells you to do something, he will never set you up for failure. Unlike humans, He is somebody who keeps His word. Just like Abraham believed in God, we need to believe in Him because whatever He promises, He can perform. God told me to go to college, and that's what I was doing!

I won't pretend it was easy. God had worked out many of the practical details of my education, but it was still up to me to study and do assignments and manage two hyperactive, out-of-control children on my own. It took a lot of effort and work on my part to make God's plan a reality. As glad as I was that I was finally putting my life in order ... I often felt incredibly alone.

I started going to church. Living Faith Outreach (in Dickenson, Texas) would be my church home for the next eight years. The pastors there, John and Jeana Gilligan, were like second parents to me; they made sure I stayed on the straight and narrow. I would often get phone calls from different church members to make sure I was all right and didn't need anything. I made it my mission to be at every service in 2000. I would always bring carloads of women from the shelter with me. I am proud to say that I helped many friends from the shelter to give their lives to God.

I was continuing my education at Alvin Community College, but transportation was an issue. So, my pastor's wife, Jeana, offered to drive me to school. While this was an incredible blessing, I knew that it wasn't right to let her put herself out so much. I didn't have any other options though, so I prayed about it and hoped God would show me a way to make this work.

Shortly after I put this issue on my prayer list, God took care of it. It is incredible how He can take care of so many things if you just trust him with your concerns. On one of the drives, Pastor Jeana told me that the church was going to buy me a car. They were true to their word and bought me a vehicle.

It wasn't anything new or flashy; it was definitely a fixer-upper. It didn't matter to me, though, I was just so happy to have it. With a car, I would be able to get a job and afford a place to live.

While I was glad I had a car finally, it did not solve all my problems right away. The search for a job was very discouraging; between my background check and college hours, no one was interested in hiring me. Wherever I went, my past followed me. As I continued to look for a job with no results, I started getting nervous. I wanted to leave the shelter, and I couldn't do that without a job.

After a few weeks of futile searching, I began to pray. I was tempted to dance again just to get out of the shelter; Satan whispered in my ear that it was the only way. I prayed to God to help me find another way because I knew I was not going to go down that road again.

Again, He answered. Not with a call-back to any of the places I had applied, but in His own way. People at church started to approach me with work they needed done, from house cleaning to fixing things in their homes. I took every opportunity that presented itself. After I left their houses, church members would sometimes bless me with a hundred dollars more than what my service required. I was definitely pulling in enough money along with my financial aid from school; I would be able to get a place for me and the kids.

I found a cheap apartment close to the school. It was definitely one of the cheapest in the town of Alvin, but I wanted to make sure I could walk to school if I had car trouble. I worried about not having furniture, but one day (to my surprise), I found that my apartment was full of furniture. I knew the church was coming by because I had left the door open for some of the members who had offered to stop by with some things. I didn't realize that they would be so generous. I will never forget my denim couch; it was the nicest piece of furniture I had since I stopped dancing. When I sat on that couch, I felt as if things weren't so bad, like my life might even get better. I continued to work hard at my classes, take care of my children, and pray for a better life for Cameron, Cindy, and myself.

One of my greatest sources of strength at that point in my life were the women from my church who constantly called and checked up on me. That church family was an honest reflection of God at work in the world. I have yet to see another church family who invested as much time and effort in me as this one had done. Ms. Dylis, the administrator of the church and principal of the private school, took time out to disciple me. She prepared Bible study sessions for me and talked with me every week about growing with God and how to face the struggles in my life. She also gave parenting advice and tips. The people at my church knew how much of a mess I was and yet, they prayed for me, watched out for me, and offered support without judgment.

People seem to know when they are being judged, and it drives a wedge between the person being judged and what God wants to do for them. That's why Jesus told us not to judge lest we ourselves be judged. We do not want to suffer God's wrath for the things we have done. Even those who have led a so-called "good life," without accepting Jesus, ultimately are lost. Passing judgment on the lost is useless because they are lost, and it will make no difference. We are called to seek them out and save them, but it's only through the power of God and the blood of Jesus that any can be saved.

After living in that apartment for a year, I made friends in the town of Alvin. Although my church family offered me a great deal of support and comfort, I was still a young woman who needed to hang around with other young women. This is when I met April and Mandy, my neighbors. They lived a few doors down. Sometimes, we would barbecue on the weekends. When we were done eating, they would go to a local bar where they could karaoke for the night. This seemed like harmless fun until I realized that April and Mandy were both doing ecstasy.

It now seems obvious, and yet I had been overlooking the signs because I had wanted to block out that aspect of my past. It filled me with disappointment, but I continued to hang out with them for the last month of my lease. April had introduced me to this guy named Jason; I really liked him, and he seemed to like me too. I thought that maybe I had found a permanent boyfriend, and then I found out he had his own demons: I learned he shot up. This was more than a turnoff; this frightened me a lot, so I broke our budding relationship off immediately. He responded by threatening to kill my children and me. I was scared; I recognized this kind of dangerous behavior. Jason was just like my father, and I didn't want anyone like that anywhere near my children.

When Pastor Jeana found out that about the type of people I was hanging out with, she gave me the reminder I needed. She reminded me of what I had told her about God's message to me, and she said the words again, "Make a choice." She was right. I just needed some reminding. I was twenty-five now, and I needed to make better choices.

The church offered another great source of support for me during this rough transition: a Bible study group called Esther. After seeing signs of my depression, Lynn, a church member who was also a nurse, decided to start the Esther group. The group would meet once a month and have a Bible study fellowship. This was a great outlet for women who attended, and it was exactly what I needed. We could talk about anything and everything, and the best part was that there was childcare. Esther group was God's solution to my boredom and loneliness; it gave me the opportunity to be social with people who would support and encourage my faith and healthy lifestyle.

12. The Turning Point

After my apartment lease was up, I moved back to a shelter. The Bay Area Turning Point was to be my home for the next six months, but I was surprised when I actually saw it – it was nothing like the others.

This had to be the nicest shelter I had ever seen. The location was kept a secret so that women who lived there would be safe from their abusive spouses. The shelter's whole mission was to provide recovery solutions for survivors of family violence and sexual assault. As part of that, the shelter introduced residents to violence-prevention strategies as a way to effect societal change. This was the perfect place for me.

Living in a shelter is never easy. While you gain a roof over your head and the opportunity to learn new things, you also have to pay attention to the shelter's rules and deal with many people who you don't know very well, on a daily basis. These women and children were hurting, and while I felt for them deeply, abused women can be angry and difficult. The strangest thing I encountered is that some women would gang up on others. Not in the traditional sense; they wouldn't get together and physically attack the other women; they would just band together to do rude and hurtful things to them (and sometimes even to their children).

It was troubling to see hurt women strike out at other abused women; the abused was now the abuser. The Turning Point staff managed these situations well; they were constantly aware of this type of behavior and nipped such behavior in the bud whenever possible.

The shelter offered many opportunities for women to grow; we learned about the cycle of abuse and how to recognize abusive behaviors. The shelter also offered many different services: group therapy, transportation, schooling assistance, childcare, legal help, medical service, and so much more. There, I learned to take control of my own actions and live up to my responsibilities.

All the girls at the shelter loved to barbecue at Clear Lake Park in the Greater Bay Area of Houston. It was a beautiful park next to the water; it was a good place to get away from daily pressures and forget about what events in the outside world had brought us together. On Saturday, the girls and I went to our usual spot in the park. But this time, we decided to bring along some beer. We were all having a good time chatting about our lives when I saw one girl we hadn't invited. We didn't do so because this girl seemed to enjoy getting people in trouble. As soon as I saw her, I knew we were in trouble. It was only a matter of time before everyone attending the barbecue would have to find another place to live. All of us had signed a contract saying that we would not drink or do drugs while we were living there, and we had clearly broken that contract.

For the rest of that day, we were all scared. Nothing really happened until the following day when the staff began calling us in for interviews. When it was my turn and I saw the look on my caseworker's face, I knew all bets were off. I am a horrible liar. Even when I am keeping a secret, I can only do so until someone asks me about it because I can't lie about the secret. It wasn't hard for my caseworker to get answers; she just asked me to tell her about our barbecues. I immediately told her everything, but I didn't mention other names. I followed the code of the streets and wouldn't rat out my crew; at that time in my life, these girls were my family. I did tell my caseworker that I would attend some AA meetings; I knew it wasn't acceptable to put my family's well-being in jeopardy just for a good time. My caseworker told me how disappointed she was and that she would talk to the board about what should be done.

For the next few days, no one would talk to me. They knew I had ratted myself out, and they were sure I had done the same to them. Each of the other girls, when interviewed about our outing, denied ever doing anything. A day or so later, someone had poured bleach all over my clothes. I guess someone thought I was tattling even though I never did.

The next day, I was called back in by my caseworker. I was scared of what she might have to say about me. To my utter surprise, she told me how proud she was of me for being the only one to tell the truth and for agreeing to go to AA meetings.

This honesty of mine was precisely what made them think of giving me another chance rather than throwing me out. However, they also made it clear that there would be strict rules in place this time. I had never been more grateful than I was then, because God had granted me another chance. I began to take my life more seriously and accept what I needed to learn from Bay Area Turning Point.

I couldn't wait for the day that I could give back to the shelter that has given me so much. All shelters could use extra help, even ones as great as Bay Area Turning Point. You don't always have to give money, but you can pick up an extra roll of toilet paper or paper towels, diapers, food, and clothes. All these things will help your local shelter. You have to understand that these places provide every single need for these families, and they could use your help.

After thirty days of being at the shelter, I was able to get into transitional housing in the Pasadena area with a recommendation from my caseworker; there were just two requirements. First, the resident needed to have transportation. Unfortunately, my fixer-upper Ford had broken down recently. This was terrible timing – without a car, I didn't know how I was going to get a place to live or how I would get to my classes.

The car had needed repairs before, and my church family had stepped in. Lynn, the nurse that headed the Esther group, had her husband do the work on the Ford anytime there was a problem. This particular time, however, Lynn's husband was working extra hours and couldn't find time to fix my car. To my huge surprise, the two of them gave me a vehicle instead. It was a Geo Tracker, and I loved it! It was green, nearly new, and awesome. Shortly after they gave it to me, I found out that they were financing this truck for me. I couldn't believe it; they paid the note on this wonderful piece of transportation for a year until I was able to pay it off myself. I pray blessings over their life all the time, and I thank God for putting them in my life.

The next thing I needed in order to move into this transitional housing was: either have a job or be enrolled in school. I had both. I had my house-cleaning business, so I had an income. It worked out great; I moved out of the shelter and into the transitional housing in November 2000. For the first time in a long time, I was happy.

13. The Gruesome Twosome

The "gruesome twosome" was the name I gave my two children, Cameron and Cindy. While I loved them beyond imagination, they were out of control. They could tear up a house quicker than a 'New York minute'. I would try to get waitressing jobs during the day – something more than cleaning houses. After the second or third day, the childcare centers would call me at work. I would have to leave work when they called because they just couldn't handle my children.

I thought that over time, their behavior would settle down. It didn't. I was running short on money, and this fear was beginning to catch up with me. I had bills to pay, and I still needed to go to school. I began to get depressed.

After all that happened and all that time and effort I spent getting out of that hole, I am embarrassed to say that I started drinking again. This time, I was able to limit the number of drinks I had to three or four – to wind down at the end of the day. But this was no excuse. I was back to using alcohol as a tool to sedate myself from all the stress.

The problems with Cameron and Cindy existed regardless of who took care of them. Cameron cried and banged his head. He was always fine when he was with me, but when I left him, he would become inconsolable and refused to behave when he was left with someone else. I cried so many times over the pain I knew he was feeling and because I felt powerless to help him. There was nothing I could do.

The rash behavior of my four-year-old son was becoming a nightmare. Cameron would constantly get into situations where he would try to purposefully hurt himself. Was he self-sabotaging at the tender age of 4?

What had I done to him? I couldn't help but blame myself. I had used drugs while pregnant. I had hurt my child and couldn't fix it. I was the one unable to get a strong enough grip on my life. I felt unable to give my children the kind of life they deserved, one where I was always available to them and the main thing to worry about would be deciding which cereal to have for breakfast.

I cried out to God for my son. I often sobbed and ached. Things got so bad that I had to hospitalize my four-year-old son. The psychologists told me that his behavioral issues were indeed his attempts of self-sabotaging himself. He was suicidal! He was in a children's psychiatric ward for seven days.

His sister Cindy wasn't doing that well, either. She had her own issues. She was generally loving and sweet but sometimes, she had anger issues. There were times she would swear that I had said something I never did. I loved and comforted her, but I really had to concentrate on Cameron. He needed me more; he kept trying to hurt himself. Perhaps, my extra attention towards Cameron made Cindy feel threatened, jealous and insecure; did she feel that she never had mommy to herself as much as her brother did?

My kids went on with their issues, but time does not stop for anyone, right? After about six months, I received public housing and moved into a new apartment. Public housing was different than Transitional Housing. Transitional Housing had strict rules concerning men and curfews. There were meetings that we had to attend and weekly apartment inspections. Only women who came out of shelter were able to go to the transitional housing. In Public Housing, it was your own choice where you would live, and there were no strict guidelines. I was happy to be on my own. The transitional housing was a great support, but we weren't allowed to have male friends stay. Even with all the things God had done for me – saving my life, paying for my college, giving me a place to live, and blessing me with two beautiful children – I still had a huge hole in my heart. At the time, I thought this hole indicated a need for attention and love from a man. This need for a manly figure – which had been there since childhood – which had brought me down many wrong paths over my lifetime – was rising again inside me.

It did not help that my children were getting old enough to ask where their fathers were. I never thought about the effects of having children out of wedlock while pregnant or when my two kids were younger. But as the years went by, I could see that it was more damaging on the children than I could ever have imagined.

So, what did I do when my children asked me where their father is? I always told them that they didn't have a dad, but they have a mother that loves them more than anything. But nothing could satisfy a child's need for their father. There were not enough words in the world that I could say to my children to make up for not having a father. I know that some single parents take on the responsibility of both, but have you been following my story so far? Take a look at my life and tell me if I was capable of assuming the role of both mom *and* a dad to Cameron and Cindy? Other single mothers had other adults around like aunts or grandparents to help out, to give children extra attention. My kids had no one but me, someone whose parenting skills still needed work. Raising children alone is just plain hard.

All I could do was to just tell my kids that they didn't have a dad, but they still had me. This went on for some time until someone at Cindy's daycare said that everyone had a father and asked Cindy about hers. How dare the daycare people contradict what I told my kids! They had no right.

Unfortunately, my little girl would not let it go. Cindy wouldn't stop pestering me about it. She was only three, and her heart ached for something she would never have, a father. I couldn't really blame her. I decided to do something about it and start dating again. This time, I vowed to make it work. My intentions would be out on the table, and I wouldn't allow any man to waste my time. I wanted a husband!

My first date was with a guy named Darren. When he came to my house, he seemed happy to meet Cameron and Cindy. The first thing out of my little girl's mouth was, "Are you my daddy?" I thought I was going to die. Darren just smiled.

"I am so sorry," I said. I am a dark-skinned girl, but my face must have turned red.

To make matters worse, Cameron and Cindy started jumping up and down chanting, "Our daddy, our daddy, our daddy." I was mortified. I needed death to come at that very moment. Of course, that didn't happen; that would have been too easy. I just had to suffer through it.

All I could do was apologize, and he assured me it was okay, but he never called again.

The next time I went out, I made sure the guy would not meet my kids right away. My heart hurt for my children; I felt that the chances of finding a decent person who wanted to date someone with two children would be slim. I knew they wanted a daddy even more than I wanted a husband.

My children's issues became more obvious and as their behavior got worse; leaving them with sitters and daycare was getting more difficult. I did not understand their issues; I thought they were just being bad. It took me years to understand that I was all they had, no father, no visits with family members, just me. I was *their everything*!

I decided that I can't blame my circumstances for preventing me from being the best possible parent I could be to my children. I was not being a good example of God's love for them. I was too busy trying to find love for myself, someone to love me. So, while I was on a mission to find a father for my children, I was ignoring the Heavenly Father and making things worse by trying to fix them myself.

During these times my mind often wandered to Hester and her relationship with Pearl. She didn't have a husband either, Pearl didn't have a father. To make matters worse, their lives were a part of a society where the only thing women were allowed to do was hide in their husbands' shadows. If Hester could survive those circumstances, what is my excuse? I made myself a promise to hold myself more accountable for my children's well-being.

I would try harder to be the mom that my kids deserve.

I've often heard it said that parenting never comes with an instruction book, so, sometimes, you have to go out and buy one. That is exactly what I did. I started asking questions, went to parenting classes, and bought books. I began to search out the parents of well-behaved children to find out what they were doing differently. Most of these parents were married. This made sense; this was how God set up the family to be: a joint effort in raising children. It was only logical that it would be easier if you followed God's plan.

There was nothing I could do about being a single mother, but I had to rethink some of the things I did with my children that weren't working. After all, they were created by God, from me. Why wouldn't I want something from me to be good? Other parents said that the children emulate what they see their parents do. I needed to be a better example. The first thing I would do is find a good job.

I also began reading the parenting books I had bought. Every one of them strongly advised setting a schedule. I put together a detailed schedule for my children. It started from the time they awoke and went through the day, until bedtime. It took a couple of weeks for us to learn the schedule, but when we did, things started to turn around. Even my behavior began improving. I wasn't as stressed out anymore over everything. I didn't feel the need to drink anymore during this year, and we began to flourish as a family. I no longer called my children the gruesome twosome; they were now the dynamic duo.

14. Job Hunt vs. Husband Hunt

As much as I loved the Lord and my children, at the age of 27, I felt that I was still missing something in my life. I assumed that it was the most obvious thing: being single. My children were wonderful. Cameron and Cindy made me laugh and kept me from wanting to do drugs; I wanted to see them happy and healthy. I also felt like I needed something for me, so I began to look for a different job. I was blessed by the houses I cleaned, but I longed to do something more meaningful. What could I do? I didn't have any talents that I knew about.

I had an interview with a local food chain for a management position, and it went very well. I was essentially promised the job as long as I passed the background check. I couldn't pass a background check, of course. When they ran the check, each of my arrests came up. The worst thing was the prostitution. I explained to the district manager that it was dismissed due to mistaken identity and that the whole thing actually had nothing to do with me. He said the fact that it was there, raised issues, and he decided not to hire me because of it. I began to get depressed again. I wanted to rip this letter from my chest and remove the mark of Cain from my head. The thought of never being able to get a decent job broke my heart. It felt as if there was a glass roof above my head, and I would never be able to break through it. I began to think that if maybe I could find true love, I wouldn't have to worry as much about having a great and meaningful career.

I continued to date different guys; my neighbor Connie would keep my children, so I could go on dates. For the most part, the kids behaved on these nights; it helped that I would wait until after bedtime to go out. I started seeing Mike regularly; he was a single father with a daughter. I thought it sexy to see a guy manning up and taking such good care of his daughter. Mike and I got along great, except that he liked to flirt with other women in front of me. I later learned that he did the same thing to his ex-girlfriend (currently in jail). I hung out with him for about six months. But when he told me his baby's mama was getting out of jail and he was going to be with her, I didn't have to be told that things between us were now over.

After Mike said that his ex-girlfriend was bisexual and "would really like me," I saw what he was hinting at.

"Mike," I said, "Do you seriously believe that the three of us together are going to be one big happy family?"

"I was hoping we could." Mike said it with so much conviction. Like it could happen. My kids, his kid, her, him, and me. Jerk!

Despite this, I liked Mike's friends. They were young, successful and had promising futures; I wanted these things too. As much as I liked my church friends, they were older and married (and had other married friends). I didn't exactly fit in. Connie had become my best friend; she shared my habit of dating the wrong men. At this point in my life, God had taken away drugs and partying.

However, I still had issues about wanting to feel loved at any cost. I wanted to be enough for someone. I had a God-given need that was perverted by Satan. I hated being lonely and unmarried. Meanwhile, I continued the job hunt and took a job at the Waffle House. The Waffle House wanted me to be a shift manager, but the hours were bad, and I just couldn't leave my children at night anymore. I would also have to quit school, and that simply was not an option. If I quit school, I would always be struggling.

When someone told me that there were openings in the Houston school district for substitute teachers, I decided to apply. This was the job of my dreams: a professional job I could be proud of ... a job which my children would be able to respect. I applied, but I didn't get the job; I assumed that the background check and my limited job history had something to do with it.

The Universe was again reminding me that my background would remain my scarlet letter, announcing to everyone that I was not to be trusted – scaring everybody away before I had a chance to prove differently.

Not being able to get a job did not make me feel good about myself, but I had to keep trying. Giving up wasn't an option. My mother had raised us to be independent; I, the oldest, was the only one who could not catch a break. After all, God had forgiven me and paid for my college; if He was on my side, no one could be against me. Every time I felt hope beginning to fade from my heart, I would remind myself of God's love and support. He already took me away from so much misery; surely, He must have thought about the rest of my journey as well.

I regularly reminded myself of this as I worked on improving my life. They say that when you have God by your side, you don't need anyone else. And if He was truly on my side, these hard times were just a hiccup. Determination had become my new friend. Little did I know how much assistance I would later be needing from this new friend.

15. A Marriage Made in Hell

The scarlet letter on my chest made it very difficult to stay positive and determined. The more I tried tearing it off, the more the adhesive stuck to me. No matter where I went, my past was on my tail.

The job hunt continued terribly, I went on at least eight interviews in a row without a single callback. The worst part was waiting for the phone to ring because all I could do was sit there, hopeful but knowing that my chances were slim. Some companies were nice enough to send me a postcard, saying something like, "Thanks for applying but we have filled the position." What they really meant to say was, "Thanks for applying. You gave us a good laugh, but don't bother coming back, we aren't interested in people like you."

At least that's what it felt like. I wondered if anyone would ever forgive me for making bad decisions for two years of my life. Or would this bad luck never end?

While I was wallowing in self-pity over my failed attempts to find employment, I was still hanging out with friends of Mike (the single father with the wandering eye and locked-up girlfriend). They had become my friends while we dated and stayed that way even after Mike and I were finished. One day, when we were all hanging out at a pool hall, I saw a guy that really caught my attention. Our eyes connected; I knew I needed to talk to him and he wanted to talk to me.

He couldn't take his eyes off me, and I wanted to put my hands all over him. He kept staring but didn't make any moves to come over and talk. By this time, my determination and assertive attitude applied not only to the job hunt, but also the husband hunt. I couldn't wait for him to make the first move. On my way to get another drink, I walked straight up to him and asked him, "Are you going to say something to me, or just stare?"

"Aren't you with Mike?" he asked.

That was the common assumption because I still hung out with his crew.

"I am trying to get with you. Good pick-up line, huh?"

We both started laughing. After a while, my friends wanted to know what was so darn funny.

"I never had a chick throw *me* a pick-up line before."

We laughed some more.

"So, you're not with Mike," he said cautiously.

"Na, but he did offer to move me in with his baby mama who just got out of jail."

"Whaaat?"

"Nope, not dating anymore. Do you have any baby mamas in jail anywhere?"

"Nope."

"Girlfriends, wives?"

"I have only had two girlfriends, and that was years ago," he said.

"How old are you?"

"27."

"Me too," I said. "So, you mean to tell me that you are 27 and don't have any children?"

"Na, no children. I don't think I can have any. I want some, though."

Poor guy didn't even know – those were the magic words! He was starting to look even better to me.

He introduced himself as Matthew. The more we talked, the more he seemed like a real catch. He was easy to converse with. I told Matthew about my children, and he said he would be stoked to meet them. I was usually nervous about bringing others around my family because I knew Cameron and Cindy would drive them up the wall. It had happened so many times before.

Well, I thought, if they scared him off, then he wasn't the man for me. The Man of My Dreams would always have to get my children's approval.

Matthew admitted that he had seen me once before and a mutual friend had told him I was Mike's girl. I laughed when I realized who the "mutual friend" was. It was Brian, another friend who had wanted to get with me for as long as I could remember. Brian had known that Mike and I had broken up, but he probably was afraid of ruining his own chances. When I explained this to Matthew, we had a good laugh. Later, we exchanged phone numbers and set up a date.

I was so excited about my upcoming date, but I kept wondering if Matthew was as cute as I remembered. He was a Latino man with a brown glow and a broad, muscular chest. A few days later, when I met him for our much-anticipated date, I realized he was even better looking than I had originally thought!

This was definitely love at first sight ... or was it lust? Either way, I was incredibly attracted to him. Matthew was funny; we played pool and went back to my house for a few beers. I figured it was okay since my children were asleep. We never once talked about God, our beliefs, or what we wanted out of life. We just slept together. I told myself he was the one, but I was settling. I wanted a man, and he was interested in me; so I went for him – even though I knew it was wrong.

The next morning Cindy met me in my room. Usually, I was careful enough to make sure any man who stayed the night would be gone by the time my children awoke. Not this time – Cindy came into my room and found Matthew. She had a million and one questions for him, including the dreadful, "Are you my daddy?" I was sure this would be that last time I ever saw Matthew. Instead, he laughed extremely hard. Cindy just stood there, looking, waiting for the answer she never got.

After that day, Matthew was a part of our family; Cindy fell in love just like I did. Matthew was usually playful with the kids and helpful around the house, but he had an ugly side as well.

The closer you get to people, the more you can see them for who they really are – and not as you want them to be.

I soon got to know that Matthew had a drinking problem. Anytime Matthew drank too much, he would become terrifying. He would have violent outbursts, scaring me, Cindy and Cameron. He would also destroy things around the house, particularly things that my family had given to me. I would throw him out of the home, but the next day, he would return full of apologies and claims that he didn't remember what had happened the night before. He would talk about how much he missed the kids, and Cindy would be crying for him. I would cave in and give him another chance because I wanted to believe that he could become the husband and father I wanted so badly.

I had a dream of a perfect family, with a husband who took care of my children, brought home flowers, and most importantly, loved both my children and me. I hoped that giving him another chance would allow Matthew to become the kind of man I had dreamt about.

I loved Matthew, and I always wanted to believe that he would change for us. Cindy and Cameron were inspirations for me to change; maybe the three of us could do the same for Matthew.

What I failed to see was that Cindy and Cameron made me change because they were my blood. But Matthew wouldn't share the same kind of bond.

Like any other woman in love, desperate to find love in a man who was basically a lost cause, I tried to change Matthew. He would make promises to behave differently, and I wanted to believe him, just like my mom believed my dad after each of his Friday-night outbursts.

But just like my father, he never changed. You should know: If you are waiting for a guy to change his ways, if you feel that your love for him will somehow be reason enough for him to change, you are deceiving yourself. Over the years, I have realized that true change comes only when the person wants to change their ways, not when someone else wants him or her to do so.

For women who are hurt by the men they are in love with, remember: ultimately it is a man's actions – not his words – which you must look at. A man's pretty words and empty promises will do little for you – and can even leave you with nothing.

Still, I was desperate to have a man in my life and have a father for my kids. Through my church and on my own, I had been reading the Bible regularly. As I thought about Matthew, a passage from *2 Corinthians* ran through my mind. "Do not be yoked together with unbelievers. For what do righteousness and wickedness have in common?" (*2 Corinthians 6:14*)

I knew that God was telling me not to stay with Matthew. Matthew was not righteous. As a woman trying to be righteous, I should have fled from a man who was not interested in seeking a better path. But I couldn't get my mind right; I felt I needed someone to love me ... and that someone had to be Matthew.

Although it was clear that we had very different ideas about how a family should behave, when I got pregnant, we decided to get married. I was tired of having children out of wedlock, and I certainly did not want to have another abortion. I married Matthew, and while I was busy doing that, I flunked out of school.

I prayed for God to show me Matthew's heart, and He did, even though it wasn't what I wanted or expected. Matthew disappeared right before our marriage. That wasn't what I meant! I wanted God to show me the good in Matthew, but apparently, God thought it was better that I see the real Matthew. His disappearance before the wedding was disappointing, but it wasn't the only time. Matthew was always disappearing. He would pop into and out of my life without explanation or apology. I was stubborn and needy; I was afraid of being alone again especially because I had three children too. Overlooking Matthew's faults (and God's obvious message), I married him anyway.

My fear of being alone was deeper than my trust in the Lord.

Every part of our relationship and marriage was stressful, especially while I was pregnant. I thought being pregnant would make Matthew straighten up, but things did not improve. I was not making enough money, and Matthew was an unreliable source of income. He often didn't work, and when he did manage to find a job, he would disappear on payday. While he was away, he would miss work and lose the job, starting the cycle all over again. My family was now bigger, I couldn't make ends meet, and I was overwhelmed. How would I be able to fulfill God's plan for my life?

My life was going so poorly again, and I became certain that it was because I had messed up badly. I feared that I would never fulfill my potential as God had intended. Throughout my marriage, I often prayed for the Lord to show me my husband's heart. Each time I prayed for him, Matthew would disappear for a day or two. It soon became clear that it was God my heart longed for. Only God could bring healing to my wounded heart.

16. God's Purpose: What He Really Wanted from Me

At certain points in our lives, we wonder about our purpose in this world. Is our existence meaningless? Is there more to our identity? Sometimes, it takes years (or even decades) for some kind of purpose to find its way to us. And even when we find it, we don't always know what to do with it.

It can take months or years before that purpose is even a possibility. When I was young, God showed me that I would fulfill my purpose by ministering to thousands of young people. I believed it then, but as my life took me in so many wrong directions, I lost sight of that purpose.

God did not forget. He never does.

After falling out of college, giving birth to two more children, and still being unable to find a decent job, life was looking particularly grim. I was tired of cleaning houses and waiting tables. I knew I had made a mess of things and ruined the chance at college that God had so carefully arranged for me. But I hoped that He could still use me in some way.

I was asking a lot, considering all my failures were my own fault. God even told me not to marry Matthew, and I did it anyway!

What was I going to do about my life now? I was ready to make a change and put my life back in God's hands, but my life was a mess. My children were having major behavioral issues again: Cindy was even hearing voices. I took her to a psychiatrist who diagnosed her with bipolar disorder. My poor baby! I couldn't feel like this was all my doing.

In a way it was ….

I needed a job. Ms. Lynn had resigned as the head of our single mom's group because of family issues, leaving me without my former source of guidance and release. To top it off, my husband was crazy. I felt my whole world was caving in and I was going to break at any second. I couldn't see a plan for my life anywhere.

Then God gave me peace.

Generally, my communication with God involved asking a question and God giving me an answer – even if that answer was a no. At other times, God gave me a command without asking first (such as the time he told me to go to school and the time he told me I had to make a choice).

This time, however, the message was more subtle, and came through Connie, one of His servants who also was my friend.

One day, Connie told me how she had just gotten a job with a school in Houston. I was happy for her, but I was also envious because I was having such a difficult time getting a respectable job. I had really wanted to work as a substitute teacher and was incredibly disappointed when my background check disallowed me from being hired.

It was difficult for me not to feel slighted, even though Connie was usually nice to me.

Connie had always been open and honest with me, so I told her about my issues with the background check. She told me, "Everyone makes mistakes and you are not a felon. Call them up and make an appointment to see the head of human resources. Explain the situation. The worst they can do is say no."

"No," I replied. "The worst thing they can do is kick me out and file a restraining order."

Actually though, I ended up taking Connie's advice anyway.

When I called human resources, they told me to apply. I also let them know that I had applied two years ago, but was never hired. The woman on the line was understanding and helpful. She checked my previous application and found I was denied employment due to a negative background check. This was no surprise to me. She asked me if I would like to speak to the head of human resources, and I said that I would.

She connected my call to Mr. Mennis, the head of human resources. He picked up the phone and said, "Mennis here. How may I help you?"

I explained that I had previously applied for a substitute teacher but had not been hired because of a negative background check. I was honest about everything to Mr. Mennis. I told him that I knew I had messed up in the past and that I was no longer that person who I was a long time ago. I told him that I wanted the opportunity to work for his district and that it would be a dream come true. I also explained how the charge of prostitution was a mistaken identity charge and that the charges had been dropped.

"Well," Mr. Mennis said, "I need you to fill out another application. This time I need you to list every offense and arrest that you have ever had. After you submit your application, just check at the front to see the status of your application." He was so polite. There was no judgment in his voice. I think he actually believed me.

"Thank you, sir, I will."

I wasn't sure if I would go through with the application or not; I was scared of being rejected yet again. I told myself to get over this fear and stop letting fear and weakness hold the reins of my life. Then I went up to human resources right away and got an application before I could convince myself not to do it. I listed every arrest, and I didn't have enough room to explain all of them; I even had to write on the back. These people are going to tear this thing up in my face, I thought. I was afraid I would never get a decent job and would be doomed to a life of welfare. I wanted so much more for me and my children.

The week after I spoke to Mr. Mennis, I received a postcard inviting me to a substitute orientation. Unsure of how to interpret this, I called human resources. The person explained that I wasn't hired yet and that the postcards were mailed out before background checks were completed. I was glad that I had already made it further than last time.

A few days later, I was getting ready to attend orientation. I was excited. Although I didn't really have good interviewing clothes, I remembered a nice outfit which my mother had given me a while back. I washed and ironed the outfit; as I went to the closet to look for things to go with it, the strangest thing happened.

I became aware of some familiar symptoms. Could it be? One pregnancy test later, I learned that sure enough, I was pregnant again. This would be my fourth child (and my second with Matthew). I loved babies, and I loved each of my children, but how could I afford to raise another child? Things with Matthew were not going well, but my relationship with the Lord was growing strong. I prayed for my family and husband. I hoped that God would change Matthew's heart and deliver him from his deep-seated anger. I longed for him to love us as a father and husband should. I hoped that God would make everything better. In fact, things only got worse.

While things were rocky with family life, I had managed to start substitute teaching. My first assignment was at a junior high school. From the moment I walked through the school door, I felt that this was exactly where I was supposed to be. Everything felt so right; it was one of the best days of my life.

There was something else I realized about this school: it was in a neighborhood I used to know well. I used to go to school in this district. Things in the area had changed, and it was no longer predominately white.

Back then, this area almost seemed like KKK headquarters. Now though, almost all the students were Hispanic.

While I was glad that the school was no longer run by the KKK, it had serious problems. The schools had gangs; the students talked back to teachers. I was someone who definitely understood the chip-on-my-shoulder routine. Although I was excited to be there, I was nervous I wouldn't be able to adapt to the school's changing demographics. The kids weren't quiet in the classrooms anymore; they spoke what they thought, good or bad.

For the next six months, I traveled around the city, working in different classrooms at different schools. During that time, I had a lot of free time between classes and I was able to do a lot of reading. Teen books were my favorite, but only the fantasy ones. I hated love stories because they seemed to be full of false hope. But fantasy books provided great stories without any real possibility that the stories could happen to me. We all know that love stories don't come true.

At one of the schools I worked at, one female student would always give me a hard time when she saw me. She was a pretty young lady, but it was as if the Lord just showed me her heart. Their teacher had left a writing assignment for her class; I read over this particular girl's work and realized the girl had talent, so I called her to stay back after class. She thought, of course, that she was in trouble, but she was taken aback to hear what I had to say. "This is good writing. Let me tell you something ... there is nothing more powerful than being beautiful and smart; those two make an unstoppable combination. Quit playin' and take care of business."

"Thanks, miss, I'll try harder."

The next day, I was working in the same school. I was pregnant with my last child. This girl who had given me so much trouble for the last couple of days, stopped me in the hall and asked me, "Have you got a name for your baby yet?"

"No, not really."

"Is it a girl or a boy?"

"It's a girl."

"Are you happy?"

I said, "Oh yeah!" I had gotten pregnant just three months after I gave birth to my last child. While I was happy, I was scared too.

I went back to the class that I was teaching. I handed out the lesson the teacher had left for her class; it was a better day with this set of students. At the end of the period, this young lady that I had had so much trouble with, handed me a sheet of paper. On the sheet of paper was a list of twenty-five names for baby girls; one of those names became the middle name of my baby girl, Kara. In fact, it was nearly her first name until I had a dream one night, and in it, the Lord told me to name her Annalisa. Was the dream actually a message from God? I'm still not certain, but it didn't seem like something I should take a chance on.

I loved my work, and I loved students like the one who gave me this list of names. I felt I was making a difference with my work, and it was great. Being a substitute teacher was awesome; this was the best job I had ever had.

17. Good Things Come to Those Who Wait

Summer was about to come. While I loved being a substitute teacher, I needed something more permanent. Now that I had spent more time in schools, I had a better idea of how things worked, and I thought being an employee already would give me a better chance at getting a full-time job. I hoped to be hired as a paraprofessional, also known as a teacher's aide. I loved being a substitute because it gave me a chance to interact with students at a variety of age levels and at a variety of schools. But I longed to work in a position where I would have a more lasting impact. Seeing the same students on a regular basis would give me that chance.

Staff members at the schools seemed so full of purpose. Like they say, the grass is always greener on the other side – their lawns were looking almost tropical to me! I thought that I would be much happier if I had a full-time position, regardless of what level or which students.

At night, I would spend time thinking about what I ought to do next at the school. Would I find a suitable full-time position? I wasn't sure. I put my faith in God, but I knew that the sins of my past could hinder my ability to get a stable, respectable job. I decided to call the head of the paraprofessionals, Ms. G., because she was the person I would have to talk to for any aide job. I was nervous and even a little afraid. What if they realized that I should never have been hired as a substitute? But if I wanted a permanent position, I had to make this call.

"Ms. G., good morning. My name is Deanna. I am a substitute teacher in the district, and I was hoping for a more permanent position."

"So, you already work for our district?"

"Yes, ma'am."

"Tell me your name again, please?"

I told her my full name, and I could hear clicks of a keyboard as she typed something in the background. I held the phone anxiously, waiting for news that could either make a future or break my heart.

"Ms. Wilson, all we need now is a current resume and a letter of interest. Then I can put you on the list."

"Which list is that?"

"The list that tells schools they can hire you."

"And that's it? I am hired?"

"Well, Ms. Wilson, you still have to interview when a school calls, and there are many names before yours on the list."

I quickly turned in the required material and continued to call Ms. G – first to make sure I had been put on the list, and then to see if I had moved up at all. After my sixth or seventh call, it was pretty obvious that I was very eager for a job. Ms. G warned me that the starting salary was only about twelve to thirteen thousand dollars a year. I didn't care; I wanted to work around other professional-types. Later I realized that I needed that job nearly as much as that job needed a person like me.

Two weeks went by, and I still hadn't heard from any schools.

Was I looking at rejection in the face again?

Panicking, I called Ms. G's offices once more, making her aware of my concerns and asking if there was a way to communicate my interest to these schools. She reminded me that I was way down on the list, but she did give me some excellent advice on how to interview.

She even invited me to do a mock interview.

"When you enter an interview," she said, "introduce yourself to everyone in the room before you are seated. Bring extra resumes so you have one for each person."

She gave several more pointers; probably the most helpful was to send a resume to every school where you wanted to work. So that's what I did. I sent a resume to all 58 schools in the district. I would accept any kind of position.

I waited a week before I received my first phone call.

I was called for an interview at an intermediate school; there were four people other than myself at the meeting. I didn't interview very well because I wasn't confident, and I failed to portray myself as a leader. All that I had practiced during the mock interview just kind of evaporated from my mind.

I thought that it would be bad to come off as a know-it-all, so when asked about being a leader, I said, "I am a follower, because leaders need someone to follow." My dumb behind. Why did I say that?

As soon as I said that, I could see the expressions of the interviewers change. I knew I had blown my chances with what I just said. Long story short, they never called.

It was a pretty stupid comment, but I didn't know what I was doing, and I wanted so badly to say the right things.

I figured the district would send a message out to other schools through their phone tree not to hire this crazy girl. I replayed the interview in my mind so many times; every time I did, a new wave of embarrassment would crash over me.

Another school called about an interview. I addressed their questions better, but they were afraid that I would hurt myself because I was pregnant.

The students would be difficult to handle because of their disabilities, and the school thought it would be too much for a pregnant woman. I completely understood their concerns, but it was still disappointing.

There were no more phone calls for the rest of the summer; I was surprised because I figured that with 58 resumes out there, statistics should have been on my side. The summer was hard; I had no income other than the SSI from Cindy's disabilities. I still received food stamps; that helped a lot but was very unpleasant to apply for. Sometimes, people in the office made me feel like I was lazy or less of an American. But I had to deal with it because I knew that without them, we would have starved.

Things at home continued to deteriorate. Cindy had frequent violent outbursts, my husband Matthew would disappear often, and had violent outbursts when he was around. My life was incredibly stressful, and I prayed all summer for just one more phone call.

No phone calls ever came.

The end of the summer finally came, and I received a postcard from the school district. They wanted to know if I would sub again, and of course, I did. If this was what God had for me, I would be happy to do it. I still wanted a paraprofessional position, but I would be grateful for whatever God gave me.

I called the district to let them know I wanted to continue substitute teaching during the approaching school year. All subs for the next school year were required to attend a day of training. I didn't mind attending. In fact, I looked forward to visiting different schools and all the reading I would be able to do that year. I had already made a list of all the books I wanted to read and even how I would find the money to pay for them.

Matthew eagerly gave me a phone message when I came home. "A school called and wanted to know if you could come interview," he said.

"Quit playin'."

"Right hand to the man." Matthew always kissed the tips of his finger and held them up in the air when trying to prove he was telling the truth.

I grabbed the paper out of his hand; it said Mr. Barns. It was for an intermediate school; I was so glad it wasn't elementary. I called Mr. Barns immediately and set up an interview for the next day.

I began to pray, "Lord, please put the right words in my mouth and put me in the right position."

The next morning came, and I looked super pregnant. There was no way to hide it. I was plump. There was no way they were going to hire me knowing I would need maternity leave right away. The only thing I could do was to convince them that I was more than qualified.

I felt nervous at the interview; classes would begin in two days, and it's unlikely that I would have another chance; having a huge watermelon sticking out of my abdomen provided another excuse for them not to hire me. As I checked in with the school's front office, I remembered that this school had been our rivals when I was in junior high school. That brought back memories of being young and stupid ... in my case, idiotically insane. When I was a junior high student, I recall being ineligible to play on sports teams because of my failing grades. I began to doubt myself again. What in the world was I doing at this place?

I was greeted by a handsome, sharply dressed man with shoes so shiny that I couldn't take my eyes off them. "Hello, Ms. Wilson. I'm Mr. Barns." I slowly lifted myself up out of my seat and followed G.Q. into an office where another man was already sitting. As the interview started, my confidence began to rise. At first, the two men seemed less interested in talking about my background and more about programs at their school.

One program was for the mentally challenged, which is the one I assumed I would be working in. The second program was a behavioral program for emotionally disturbed students. They asked me if had any background knowledge regarding these types of disabilities. "Actually," I replied, "that is what I went to school for. I received a certificate in mental health, although I have not finished my bachelor's degree yet."

That caught their attention.

"I have studied mental disorders as well as substance abuse," I continued. "I also have a daughter that is diagnosed with bipolar disorder, and she hears voices. She's too young to be diagnosed with schizophrenia, but the signs are there."

"Ms. Wilson, what can you tell me about a kid who is an average student and consistently late but never gives teachers any problems. He has over 60 absences but always attends after-school detention?"

"Mr. Barns, right?" The man nodded. "There can be many factors; you can't always go by first impressions. The fact that he passes his classes shows that he does care about his grades. I'm not racially profiling, but is he Hispanic?"

"Yes ma'am," I wasn't used to people addressing me in this way.

"Have you followed him home and to school?" I was really curious about this conundrum.

"Yes actually, he lives in town, very close." Mr. Barns seemed to be enamored by what I was saying.

"We followed him home," said the second man.

"I would also follow him to school. Just because he goes somewhere after school doesn't mean he lives there. It might just be a holding place. Also, is he staying up late playing video games or on medication which keeps him from sleeping?" My mind went back to the late night I checked on Cameron and found him wide awake in the dark – just staring at the ceiling. It had freaked me out.

They were hanging on my every word, so I kept talking, and they asked more questions. I was ready with an educated response to every question. At the end of the interview, the two principals wanted to know which program I would be interested in applying for. The answer seemed clear, so I said, "I am really interested in the adaptive behavior program."

"Okay, Ms. Wilson, we have a couple more interviews to conduct, and then we will get back to you." That was not what I wanted to hear. I wanted the job at this school. I felt desperate. I began talking. I knew I had to make a stronger case.

"Thank you so much for your time, but please, don't avoid hiring me because I'm pregnant. I have been promoted or at least offered a promotion at every job I can remember. I am loyal and hard working. This will also be my fourth child, and with each of the other three, I came back to work two weeks after I gave birth, so you don't have to worry about that. Just give me a chance."

I wasn't sure if this was professional or not, but I knew that my pregnancy must have been something they had noticed and had to consider. I needed to address these concerns head-on.

I left, not sure what was going to happen. On my way out, I saw another seated woman waiting to be interviewed. She was an older woman, probably in her late sixties or early seventies. She looked stern as if she would swat students on the hands with a ruler. I knew she was after my job, and I hoped she wasn't the type of person they were looking for.

I went home and waited all afternoon for a phone call. The phone call didn't come. I was getting off on the wrong foot with my unborn baby already, because I felt it was her fault that the phone wasn't ringing.

The next morning, I laid on the couch and refused to move. I was sad, frustrated and very pregnant. Finally, the phone rang. I could see on the Caller ID that it was the school I had interviewed at, the day before.

"This is Deanna."

"Good morning, Ms. Wilson. This is Mr. Barns. I am calling to offer you a position."

"Yes, of course!"

"Are you able to start tomorrow?"

"Yes, and what program will I be working in?"

"You said you were interested in the adaptive behavior program."

"Yes, sir, that's the one I was hoping for."

I began to dance around the apartment and sing. My family thought I had lost it. I was so happy, even happier than when I had become a substitute.

"Thank you, Lord, thank you!"

The next day I started work. The students weren't there yet; they would arrive the next day. I could hardly contain my excitement as the peer facilitator led me around the school. She was so kind, as she introduced me to all the staff, including my new supervisor, Mr. Man. He was tall and athletic and had a voice that seemed to echo around the rooms.

I wanted to do a great job. I hadn't had employment that was really meaningful since I was 19 and had worked at the world's largest Full Gospel camp. Life seemed so miraculous then, and I dared to believe anything could happen. With this new job, I was beginning to believe that maybe good things were going to come my way.

Maybe the skies were ready to clear up once and for all.

18. Best Job Ever

The first day of school came. I was excited to meet the young people in my class, and I wondered why God would grant my petition to work with hurting youth.

That first day, I could never have anticipated how my studies in mental health would be an advantage, and how my experience at summer camp had prepared me for this exact position. All the pieces of the jigsaw puzzle seemed to fall into place.

When I was younger, I knew that I had been called to work with young people. The call from God, that I had heard and understood from my youth also referred to my current role at the school. I hadn't understood this until now.

I knew my first day would be challenging, and of course, the students didn't like me or my supervisor. This was his first year in the program as well (even though he had already taught for eight years). The students were defiant, and a few could not even read because of other disabilities, causing even more behavioral issues.

Some students were smart but had ended up in this program because of questionable outside influences. Many came from single-parent homes or were being raised by a grandparent. Another common factor was parental drug or alcohol abuse, which had to affect how students acted at school. Some of these students, with the most severe behavioral issues, were either lacking consistent motherly guidance in their lives or they had stepdads with abusive tendencies. Some of my students used or sold drugs; a few even did both.

From my own life experiences, I knew the signs well, and it was easy for me to figure out what my students were doing.

When I confronted them, they responded with respect. One student, Manuel, once told me, "I wish you were my mother."

"Why would you say that, Manuel?"

"No one else cares about me, Miss."

"I would adopt you in a moment," I replied.

I told my husband about my students all the time. I told him how I wished I could adopt this student. Every now and then Matthew was a voice of reason, and this was one of those times.

"You can't just adopt everyone; you have children of your own." In my heart, I knew he was right. But as a mother, I couldn't help having maternal feelings towards my students.

These students were selected for the program because their behavior affected the learning of the general student population. Their behavior impeded the learning of other students to such a severe degree that they had to be self-contained or monitored every fifteen minutes of the school day. I was that monitor. My students were always getting into fights, usually fighting with each other but sometimes even taking a swing at the principal.

Being a teacher's aide was not easy. Sometimes, I felt I wasn't making a difference in the lives of these students. Some teachers had a hard time working with these boys. I could manage them ok, but the students with behavioral issues were a different ball game. They were like predators; only the strong would survive. With my pregnancy, their constant fights often took a toll on me.

I often would ask the Lord to lead me about these boys. Why did He allow me to get a job here? How should I deal with them? An answer began to ring over and over in my head, "Just love them." That's what I began to do. I prayed for them every morning and talked to them as if I were their mother. Their response to me was amazing.

At work, I believed things were getting better.

At home, things had become volatile and dangerous. When I first met my husband, he had promised me the world, but now, all he gave me was a headache. I married someone just like my stepfather, and Matthew had taken control of my home. He was unable to keep a job. He was stubborn and irrational, and if he didn't get his way, he would make us pay. He would go into fits of rage, destroying our home and smashing everything that would break, especially gifts from my mother and sister. He was particularly resentful of them. Physical abuse was all too common at our place, even during my pregnancy.

Finally, the time came for my baby to arrive. When it happened, I was so thankful she was healthy and normal.

I took maternity leave from work for just two weeks (even though six weeks was the normal allotted time). Besides, if I stayed longer at home without going to work, where would we get money to keep the house running? Also, Matthew didn't have a job. Luckily, that meant Matthew could keep both babies while I worked. However, when I was home at night, I woke up every two hours to feed the new baby and woke up again to go to work.

My supervisor and principals thought I was a saint. They thought that it was my love for the boys which made me so keen to resume work. It helped that I missed my boys. The program was interesting that way – there were only boys in my class, so that is what I called them – my boys.

While I did miss the boys at school, I knew that my eagerness to return to work had less to do with the boys and more to do with my poor financial situation at home.

When I returned, the boys were excited to see me. They wanted to see pictures; they wanted to know about the baby. I noticed that Manuel was not happy. I could see it all over his face. His face expression was that of worry. Manuel thought that the new baby would make me overlook him. My own children had looked at me the same way each time I brought home a new sibling.

I also understood this look because of an experience I had as a teenager. During those teenage years, my youth pastors were the world to me, and because I didn't have a father, Pastor John was like a surrogate dad. When they had their first baby, I was sad because I thought they could never love me as much as they did before the baby's arrival.

So, I knew exactly what Manuel was going through. But I wasn't sure how to address it.

"Miss," Manuel said to me, "We're your kids too, right, Miss?"

The classroom froze, and everyone waited for my answer. Then, it dawned upon me: Manuel wasn't the only one unsure about whether my new, cute baby would change the way I treated the class.

I didn't know how to answer, so I motioned for them to return to their desks.

Finally, I stood before the class and said, "Yes, I have kids at home, but I care about each of you as well. You are more than just students to me. I pray for you every day; at any moment, I would adopt you. I would make sure you got through college. I know each of you can make it; I want to make sure you do. So yes, you are my kids, and I love each of you. Even you, Ernie."

"Stop, Miss," Ernie said, blushing.

I wasn't lying. I really did love them.

These were my children, all of them; I wanted them to make it through this school year and more importantly, I wanted them to make it in life.

My first day back went "okay." But home was a different story; my husband was in one of his moods. Apparently, he did not exactly have a ball taking care of the kids. It is the same with all men, I think. As women, we are told from the beginning of time that a woman's job is to take care of her kids. Somehow, women seem to do so much of work and still barely get any recognition for it, especially from their partners. Our men seem to think that it is so easy staying at home, doing the dishes, doing the laundry, making food, looking after the kids, and the list goes on and on.

They seem to think that just because a woman is staying at home she does not have to do much, or the work she does is easy. It is only when you turn the tables on them by asking them to fill up just half of your shoes by taking care of the kids, that they begin to crumble under pressure.

Matthew was going through something similar.

I did not know what to do or say to him to make him feel better about things. All I could think of was to just pray and ask the Lord to show me his heart. I wanted a family with him, but I did not want my children to go through any more craziness.

They really had gone through so much already, at such young, tender ages.

That night, I cried out in repentance for all my disobedience. I cried for the Lord to show me his heart, and I swore that this time, I would listen to what the Lord told me.

19. I Saw the Sign

The same night when I had cried all my tears and prayed really hard to God, begging him to show me what to do with my husband, Matthew threw a huge tantrum. This time, it reminded me of a toddler who was not getting his way.

It was as awful as all his previous fits. As a habit, after having these fits of anger and rage, Matthew would disappear somewhere. Then he would come back, calm and incredibly apologetic, pretending not to remember what he had done. I would end up forgiving all the hurtful poison he had spewed when he was consumed by anger.

I would tell myself that we were all damaged and bruised – giving excuses to find solace in what he had done. I would say, despite our damage, we were still beautiful. I would go on to justify. "So, what if Matthew had problems? Did I not have problems of my own?" I would tell myself that if I continued judging all the men that came into my life so harshly, my kids and I would never have a shot at a decent life.

Every time he showed me his worst side, I would end up forgiving him. There would be a short period of peace until he started the cycle again with another fit of intoxicated rage.

However, this time around, Matthew's fit of rage started to look a little different. Something inside me told me that this was my sign from God, and I took action.

I called Bay Area Turning Point, because I had nowhere else to go. I wasn't sure how I would have a different life than this one, and I wasn't even fully sure that it was possible. I had made Matthew leave many times before, but we both knew he would always come back – I couldn't afford childcare and a place to live on my small salary. He knew this, of course, and it left me trapped and scared. I asked God to give me the strength that I needed.

I swore that I would never settle again. I promised that once I left Matthew, I would live a life of purity and devotion to him. It was no longer worth cheating on my Lord. Everything I said to God that day, I meant fully and still mean today.

I had already talked to the shelter, but I had to wait until it was safe to leave, because I had never left him before. The staff there helped me devise a plan. I stocked the refrigerator with his favorite beer. I made sure his pockets were full of our family's money. Then I waited because I knew I was not going to get out of the house with his children, and I could never leave the house without them. I prepared myself to endure whatever was going to happen that night because once it was over, he would leave, and we could too.

There were no angry outbursts that night, but he did sneak away. And so, did we.

I took one day off after we made our escape. Then, I went back to work. I had a message on my cell phone from the superintendent of human resources, Mr. Mennis. He was wondering why I was working for the district; he hired so many people that he must not have remembered that we had already spoken before – at great length, when I was applying to be a substitute teacher.

When I returned his phone call, he had plenty to say about my background check. He told me that he was not sure why I was allowed to be working in the school district and that we needed to have a meeting. I assured him once again that I was sorry for my mistakes and reminded him that one of the arrests was due to mistaken identity. After I explained this (and that I could not be fired for things I had already disclosed), Mr. Mennis recommended that I get these offenses expunged from my record.

In one instant, I felt like my whole existence was caving in on me. Was I going to lose my job? I loved this job even though the pay was low; I knew I belonged there, and the students needed me. When I asked him when he would like me to come in for a meeting, he told me we had just had the meeting. He apparently had said everything that he felt needed to be said and had called my supervisors to make them aware of my background check.

Mr. Barns went down to the administration building and fought for me. His efforts combined with the fact that I had fully disclosed these things prevented the district from firing me. I did find out, however, that my husband's cousin's girlfriend, Beth, was the one to alert the school. She wanted me fired because her son went to the same school that I worked at, and she believed I had been telling school staff all kinds of things about her. Beth didn't want any of her dirty laundry being revealed to strangers.

But nothing could be further from the truth. I had never said anything about Beth to the staff. I always considered her family and never would have violated her trust. Even after she led a campaign to have me removed from the job that I loved, I never told anyone about her addictions. The irony is that – one year later, she was arrested for cocaine possession, and all her problems were out in the open. I did not find pleasure in that; she had children who suffered because of her addiction. But it did strengthen my belief in the fact that God is just in all His ways.

I have learned not to try to block the Lord's work in someone else's life. I have also learned to allow God to fight my battles. These are not easy things; as humans, we think we can solve everyone's problems, but we can't. And when someone attacks you, it is human instinct to want to defend yourself. But the Bible tells us to agree with our adversaries, and that's what I did.

I had heard through the grapevine that there were rumors that I would be fired. I went to my supervisors, explained my past, and assured them that it was all in the past. At that time, it had been ten years since I was arrested for public lewdness. I knew that I was the poster child for being young and stupid, but I had changed. I had only faulted Beth for preventing me from providing for my family. God took care of the rest.

I called my mother, a police officer. She said she would help me pay to have my record expunged, so I called the district attorney's office. The assistant district attorney I spoke to was very helpful. He set me up with the right paperwork and told me what to do. It took about six months, and my record was cleared of the charge of prostitution. I was never a prostitute! Just a dancer. It made me angry that people were still getting the two confused. Now, I needed to figure out what to do with the public lewdness charge. Even with just that on my record, I felt so unworthy of being allowed to work in public education. I knew my faults, and I was scared that others would think I was a piece of three-week-old trash.

Working in education made me feel so wonderful, even if I was just an aide. Working with intelligent people made me feel a little unworthy, and I wanted to fit in with my coworkers. I never gave the impression that I thought I was better than my students or co-workers. For the first time in my life, I acted humble because I was humble. I was simply grateful for my children and my job.

During that year, our program became very successful, and my supervisors and the principals respected me. When there were problems with my class, they asked my opinion. Not only did they ask my opinion, they actually listened to me. This was a new experience for me; no one had valued my opinions before. For the first time in my life, I felt important, and this time, for all the right reasons. This time, my sense of self-worth was not tied to sex, drugs, or abuse.

This was the best job I had ever had, and I decided to go back to college and get my degree to teach. My supervisor had received a promotion to principal at another campus, and the head of my school wanted me to take over. But the district said I would first need to have a degree. That was okay with me; I was hoping it would only take a couple of years. I was so proud that the heads of my school thought that I would be a good person to lead a classroom. My life felt amazing.

I started attending classes at the College of Biblical Studies to finish my degree. This was a good arrangement for me: I would get to study the Bible and in return, I would receive an accredited degree in counseling and use it to teach. I knew I was in accordance with the perfect will of God.

There was comfort in that.

20. The Birth of Some New Ideas

Summer came, and I missed work greatly. I was really looking forward to seeing my boys at the beginning of the next school year. However, I felt like I should make the most of this time and focus on other aspects of my life.

Like, my parenting skills for example.

I bought parenting books and started reading. I also began to study the word of God concerning parenting and children. I put my two older children in counseling and began to get involved with educational and faith-based groups offered at the shelter. I went to assertiveness classes, Bible studies, parenting classes, and church.

My children were thrilled to be the top priority in my life. I didn't remember the last time they smiled or laughed. I spent more time just talking to them. I discovered that they had many different thoughts and opinions. I learned more about their likes and dislikes. They really disliked my meatloaf but ate it anyway.

Even though some of my past decisions brought so much pain and heartache, my recent decisions were shaping my way of thinking and how my children behaved. I had spent so much time trying to give them the best that I might have forgotten about giving them the thing they wanted most: me! They wanted to spend time with me. Ok, maybe pizza too, but they definitely wanted time with me.

I had spent my childhood being lonely, never feeling like I had somebody I could count on, always blaming my family for never being there. Somehow, I had ended up doing the same to my kids. Despite trying hard to prevent this from happening, it still did.

This realization broke my heart. But deep down, I knew that only God could fix this. At the age of 30, I vowed, no more! No more sleeping around. No more putting anything before my Lord. No more putting any human person before my children. No more me, just Him.

During the summer I ran into a couple of my students; they assured me they were behaving and that they were looking forward to seeing me again at school. I had hoped to run into Manuel but never did. Manuel was due to get off probation soon. My fear was that he would move back with his father (a man with issues of his own). Unless Manuel got away from such a strong negative influence, I worried that he would never get very far.

During probation, Manuel was sentenced to live with his grandmother, and she was a law-abiding citizen. The judge knew he needed stability. Manuel's brother also led him into trouble, and his brother was more likely to hang around his father. I prayed for Manuel daily.

Summer passed, and the start of school approached. The first day of school came, and there was no Manuel. The second day came; he still wasn't there. Something was wrong. My sixth sense was trying to tell me something.

I asked my supervisor about Manuel; he found out that Manuel had been arrested after getting released from probation. His older brother had talked him into breaking into a house. After learning the news, I went to the bathroom and began to cry. I stayed there for 20 minutes. This was the worst possible news. Maybe I should have tried to make contact with my students this summer. I should have tried to help his grandmother, brought food, done something to stay involved.

Over the next few months, I couldn't stop thinking about Manuel. However, life and time are cruel and wait for nobody. The year flew by, and our program was viewed as a success. Students were staying out of trouble, and my supervisor let everyone know that I was a big reason for that. The program's success even played a part in his promotion to principal. I was even doing well at my college classes (though I was eager to complete my degree).

Sometime during the summer, I took Matthew back. Soon my husband began doing his disappearing acts, which were starting to get old. One time, I placed a missing person's report because he was gone for two weeks, and I figured he was dead this time.

I needed mental support. I was raising a family, raising a husband, raising children at my job. I longed for the support that I used to get from the Esther group at church. Since it broke up, I felt really alone; with everything I had accomplished, there was still some emptiness inside me.

Previously, when this happened, it would seem like only a man's presence could fill this emptiness. And you know how that turned out! Now I knew better than to think that some man was going to make me feel whole. I was not naïve anymore.

One night during my last year in college, I had a dream that seemed so real. I had started a support group at my church that went nationwide. It was great, just like the Esther group, but with more of an outreach focus. I woke up knowing what I needed to do. I was going to restart the single moms' group.

The next Sunday after church, I went to Pastor Jeanna and asked her if I could restart the single moms' group. She said, "Deanna, I think that is a great idea, but I want you to ask Jennifer to help." Jennifer had stepped in to help the Esther group when Lynn first resigned. I was hoping she would help because she had a house and lived close to the church, while I lived 25 miles away in an apartment.

Jennifer would be an incredible asset. I called her up to invite her to help. Jennifer was excited. "Actually," she said, "that was on my heart. I just wasn't sure when to get it going."

She was happy that I had heard from God, and her enthusiasm made me confident that this is what He had intended. We discussed the ins and outs of the group and agreed that the name Esther did not describe our group. Even though I was married, I was raising my children alone.

"We have mothers raising children alone," Jennifer said.

"That's it," I said. "Mothers Raising Children Alone; we can use the acronym MRCA."

And this is how MRCA came into being. Our support group had mothers who were divorced, had husbands in jail or were grandmothers. For whatever reason, they were raising children alone and needed a way to vent.

Jennifer and I both had a grand vision of what we wanted for the group; I saw it as a big organization where both women and men could benefit from the support of one another. I wanted our group to meet once a month and talk about things we had to overcome as single parents. I wanted to produce strategies on how to stay faithful to God and stay committed to our children. I wanted to document effective methods for picking the right partner. I wanted to be involved in the lives of other parents. Regardless of how they ended up raising children alone, group members would bring a new and fresh perspective to the challenges of parenting. I needed this group, and the group needed me.

During the time that MRCA was getting started, my school was going through changes. One teacher came to work intoxicated and was subsequently fired. Rumors circulated that she had taken part in an inappropriate relationship with a former student. Her replacement was overwhelmed by the job and quit after just a few months, giving the school only 15 minutes of notice. The school was in distress over what to do.

They knew I had already passed my content test in special education but that I had not yet graduated. They pulled me into a surprise meeting and informed me that I would be teaching English language arts for the rest of the year.

The administration said that my success with the adaptive behavior program showed that I was ready for my own classroom. They let me know that there were some huge behavioral problems in this particular classroom, but due to my experience in the other program, they were confident that I could handle it. I would not be paid a regular teacher's salary but would gain the experience I needed to be hired as a teacher for next fall. I was elated! The Lord had counted me among the faithful again. Even though I was officially considered the teacher on record, I was proud to switch over from aide to teacher. I felt like I had just been included in a sacred sorority.

21. To New Beginnings

February 2nd was my first day as a new teacher. The students were rotten on purpose. They would turn their papers in written in Spanish. I would then write my comments in Spanish, telling them to write in English. I gave out many detentions that first week. They called me prejudiced and said I didn't like Mexicans. I ignored it for the first week.

The following Monday, I made sure I had a wedding picture along with pictures of my kids sitting on my desk. So, the next time I was called prejudiced, I showed that child a picture of my Hispanic husband. After that, I earned respect from some of the students. The other students were shocked when they found I understood the street lingo; in which, they said: "Don't mess with Ms. Wilson; she is gangster."

I was catching cheaters left and right. And I didn't think I was doing something particularly wonderful that no other teacher on this planet could. Didn't they understand we were all young once? Did these teenagers really think that all their teachers were born disciplined?

Nothing teaches us better than our mistakes. And in my thirty years of life, I had made several. Interestingly, every mistake I made was bigger than the last. Each new mistake hurt me more than the last; each taught a lesson greater than the last.

When they knew I wasn't going anywhere, my students began to trust me. I heard their stories and listened. Many said that I was not like the other teachers. I instilled the belief in my students that anyone could go to college, and they embraced this belief. I had guest speakers come in and talk about their struggles as they worked on college degrees. I wanted my students to believe that anyone could finish high school, attend college, and finish. They just had to find the college which was right for them.

If you work in education, remember that the kids coming to your class may be going through a lot at home. Their lives may seem confusing. They probably are surrounded by people who know just how to criticize them and nothing else. The best you could do is to offer hope and encouragement. Your teaching method should build these kids up, not break them down.

Each student in your class has potential; the teacher should help them make use of it. I used my own life as inspiration for them. Obviously, I did not tell them everything about my past, but I didn't hide the fact that I had a very rough start. If I could rise from the ashes, so could they.

At the end of the year, my students had an 80% pass percentage in the statewide test. This was very good, considering I was their third teacher that year. By the end of the year, all my students – in all seven periods had A's and B's. Some even received commendations for their test scores. I felt blessed.

The end of the school year brought anxiety about my employment for the next year. I worried that I wouldn't find a job as a certified teacher despite the assurances. I was due to graduate in three months, and I still wondered if my background would count against me. My record was expunged of some offenses, but it was still far from perfect. Just as I had done when I wanted to be an aide, I sent a resume to every single school in my district. I had only received a couple of calls back then, and I assumed it would be the same way when I was applying to be a teacher. I was wrong.

One Thursday, I took the day off to send my resumes. I sent a resume and a cover sheet to every school in our district. I delivered 11 and mailed the rest. In just a couple years, our district had grown to 77 schools. I had only gotten a few calls when I applied to be a paraprofessional. So, I expected to receive only a few phone calls now.

By the time I had gotten home from hand delivering the 11 resumes, I had already received five messages. Over the next two days, I had received so many phone calls it was crazy! When they found out I had adaptive behavior experience, principals were offering me jobs over the phone. Before I started receiving a massive number of phone calls, I had already made a verbal commitment to the first school believing it would be my only offer.

My phone rang for hours. I tried to explain to one principle that I had already made a verbal commitment to another school. She didn't care. She said, "Don't you even want to come check it out?"

"Ma'am, I have already made a verbal commitment to another principal."

"But you haven't signed a contract, right?"

"Ma'am, I am really flattered, but I have to go with integrity here on this one." I nearly had to hang up on this woman, she was so persistent. I was actually flattered that someone wanted me.

The phone calls did not stop. One afternoon, I even had to unplug the phone. I was also tired of telling people I had already found a teaching position but couldn't sign a contract until I graduated in two months.

In August 2007, I graduated from college and began teaching students with autism.

Once again, the Lord had given me favor with students as well as my supervisors. My program was blessed, and my students were learning more than I ever could have imagined. My first year as a certified teacher was wonderful. I prayed daily for my students as well as my own children.

At home, my children and I began to have weekly Bible studies and share with each other what God had done for us that week. Cameron and Cindy were growing in grace and favor. They were no longer the wild children. Also, in 2007, we discovered that God had blessed Cindy with a beautiful singing voice. I am always so proud of hearing her singing around the house. When I see what God has done for our family, joy fills my heart.

22. The Second-Best Year Ever

In 2009, my year was blessed. I received a 100% pass rate for my student's statewide assessment that year. Everyone was shocked but me. I now understood that God could do anything. One of my students with autism was reevaluated that year. The outcome of his revaluation was that he was no longer autistic. Was that possible? It was for me.

Let's just say, I said a lot of prayers for healing my students. The funny thing was that I had more students up next year for revaluation, and they would find the same thing happen with them. I wouldn't get to see it though, because I received a promotion. I was no longer a teacher, but a Behavioral Specialist for a new district.

In February 2009, 'Mothers Raising Children Alone' was incorporated and it became a non-profit organization. Our mission was to bring college educations into single-parent homes. Whether it was a guardian or child, we wanted to be able to get them through college.

I finally filed for a divorce from Matthew in March. The disappearing acts alone told me that I had a biblical reason to divorce. I grieved because I knew God hates divorce. But after going through so much pain and misery, and even after providing him with many chances to work out our differences, I never detected any willingness on his part for reconciliation. That's when I knew that parting ways was the only option.

I now trust only in God. I only seek a relationship with him. In May, I was able to be a spokesperson for Bay Area Turning Point and talk about everything they had done for me, including paying for my teaching certificate. I am blessed. My children are blessed and beautiful.

I finally decided it was time to do something about that public lewdness issue. My life had finally turned around completely, and I could not afford to have my background ruin my promising career. I filed paperwork for a Full Pardon. This would enable me to have the charge of public lewdness removed from my police record. After a few months, I received a letter in the mail. It was from the Texas Board of Pardons and Parole. They recommended me for a Full Pardon. The governor of Texas still has to sign off on it. I am just going to tread in faith. I hope he does give me one. It was a big deal for the board to recommend me because hundreds of people apply each year.

I feel honored and incredibly blessed. Like Hester Prynne, the scarlet letter on my chest no longer stood for adulteress, fornicator, harlot or anything. Like Hester, it stood for Able. God was able to complete in me everything He had started. I would be able to do everything He called me to do. The burning mess of my former life sparked flames of a new destiny. I rose out of the flames like a Phoenix.

Epilogue

Many people would recognize him on sight, although few would know his name. Even in his ragged old age, he retains those features that have made him so memorable a presence as a character actor in over a hundred films.

What you have read until now has been the story of my life so far. This life has been a collection of really bad decisions, but somehow, things ended up turning around for me.

How they turned around, you already know. I did not tell you these things to be boastful or proud, but rather because I wanted to show the incredible grace and power of God. I know that it is He who accomplished these things in me. Left to myself, I will mess everything up. I have messed up in my past more than most people I know.

Even now, there are moments where I catch myself looking at my life, overwhelmed at how things that used to be, have changed so rapidly. Sometimes I wonder if my past makes me undeserving of the blessings God has bestowed on me.

I depend on the Lord for everything, and I try to live my life as a reflection of his grace. I live to serve only him. No matter where you've been or come from, Jesus' blood was shed for you, and the forgiveness that comes with it is yours for the taking. All you have to do is reach out and take it.

We all have stories to tell and you just read mine. In this last chapter, I will document the lessons I have learned from it. They can remind you to hold onto God's rope – even when doing so seems practically impossible.

Lessons on Family

Family is where you learn about unconditional love and trust. If you have parents or siblings who love you, provide a roof over your head and protect you from all that is bad and ugly, you should consider yourself one of the privileged few. I did not have a picture-perfect family. The absence of an actual father and my subsequent efforts to seek him out in others later took a toll on me in ways that I can't imagine. If you have a father concerned about your well-being, you don't know how incredibly lucky you are. My former self would kill to trade places with you.

So, if you have a loving and supportive home, good for you. If you do not, that is not an excuse to punish yourself. There are so many people in the world, including myself, who were not dealt with all the right cards in life but still managed to work things through. Even if you have no family in this world, you have God always looking out for you.

Trust Him and His plans.

Lessons on God, Faith and Humanity

Time and again, events in my life demonstrate that if I am to trust anybody, it should be God alone. I honestly do not know where I would be or how my life would have turned out if I did not have faith in God.

Every hardship in my life has helped me to realize that nobody in this world can help you as God can. The only thing you have to do is to let God decide things for you. I have mentioned before – that as humans, we are 100% convinced that we know what is best and how to face problems that come. Reality has a way of disagreeing. For example, I actually used to think that the best way to improve my financial situation was to work at a strip club and use my body to attract paying customers.

All the hardships I faced in my life brought me closer to God. For that reason, I feel thankful that these problems found their way to me. They strengthened my faith in God and let me see my capability to overcome them.

I understand that some people may not believe in God and have personal reasons for that. As for me, I don't know what I'd do if I did not have faith in God. If I didn't have God to turn to during these darkest moments, I don't know how or even if I would have managed.

So, having faith and making time to cultivate it is very important.

Always remember your humanity. There will always be someone who could use a kind word or gesture. And if you cannot find someone to be kind to you, be that source of kindness for others. You will always be compensated for your kindness.

Lessons on Mistakes

I cannot stress this enough: you are not defined by your past. But that doesn't mean you don't have to be careful with your present.

I was used and abused in all sorts of ways, and some of it was definitely my own fault. My instances of drug abuse and public lewdness followed me for what seemed like an eternity. Those were my mistakes. They cost me heavily when trying to embark on a career. Eventually, I got past them, but those mistakes made me realize just how important it is to make decisions carefully.

Remember the time I got raped? None of the other strippers responded to Jared's call, but I did. I thought it was just going to be another opportunity to make cash. How wrong I had been! I was naïve and stupid back then, and that's precisely why those mistakes happened.

So, if you spend all your time beating yourself up about bad decisions, don't convince yourself that you are helpless and that you cannot effect change. Stop being the victim and take control of your life. For everything that happens to you, you can either run from it or stand your ground and face it.

God gave you a brain. He gave you sense and intelligence and hundreds of wonderful abilities. Use them. Learn from your mistakes and move forward with your head held up high. There are bigger and better things awaiting you; all you need is faith in God and courage to help yourself get through it.

Lessons on Love and Abuse

Most of my wrong turns were taken in the name of love. Some were inclinations brought on by previous hurt and abuse.

We all have our definitions of love and happiness. I used to think that as long as someone was physically present – if the other side of my bed wasn't empty – that meant that I was loved. It seemed not to matter if the other person had hit me or lashed out at me or made me feel less of a person.

I confused abuse for love. And that was one of the biggest tragedies of my life. I thought that being treated like trash was just a normal part of being in a loving relationship. It wasn't.

If you want to change somebody you claim to love, you really don't love them that much to begin with. My revised definition of love is accepting people as they are rather than as you want them to be. Anybody who truly loves you will never be bad for your mental health. Every relationship comes with struggles. But one person cannot be your pain and cure at the same time.

Lessons on Determination

My life also taught me that if you want amazing things to happen, you have to be patient before you start seeing the fruit of your efforts. But you will see it.

If you have a dream, you have to protect it in any way you can. Just wishing for your life to change is not enough; you have to work for it. If I had wanted, I could have remained a stripper. Or I could have let myself continue to believe that it was impossible to escape my drug addictions. But I am proud to say that I defeated that ugly sickness.

Even when things finally started going my way (like when I did substitute teaching), I was determined to go further. Resuming work only after a couple of weeks after giving birth isn't easy. But I did it. Leaving your children at home while working crazy shifts isn't easy. But I did it. Why?

Because I was and still am determined to give my family a better life. For that, I would be willing to do anything.

Phoenix

I like to think of myself as a Phoenix. The Phoenix is known for sacrificing itself to pain, suffering and even death just so it could experience a rebirth of a stronger self.

It's like the Phoenix lets itself be broken down willingly only to build itself again from scratch, with a much stronger foundation than the last time. It is my spirit animal. Like the Phoenix, I suffered. I spent an insane amount of time crying over my fate, over my luck. Good things would happen to me, only to be followed by a dozen bad things. I have been heartbroken so many times that I have literally forgotten the count. All I know is that when I look back, I can safely say that the darkest moments of my life led me to the brightest place in my life.

Just like the Phoenix, I too rose from the ashes, from my destruction and developed into a strong, independent woman who has immense faith in God.

I am happy. Seeing my children around me equally happy also gives me further strength. Devoting most of myself and my time to God and carrying out His word, gives me peace of mind and heart both. I can finally say that life is good.

You have read my story from start to finish and can probably vouch for the fact that the road to a happy life has not been an easy or a scenic one for me. But I will say that the journey is worth it – the relationship with God, the peace that comes from doing His work, and the satisfaction that comes from a life lived as He intended.

If you are also going through a rough patch, remember that things will only improve if you try to change your circumstances. Human beings are limited in their abilities, but God isn't. So even when you are trying to change your circumstances, there is only a limited amount of heavy loading that you can do. At some point, you will need God to back you up. God is not limited in any sense of the word. His wisdom, His love, and His assistance know no bounds.

All you have to do is to ask Him for help. No matter how many times you feel you have disappointed God, just find your way back to Him. There is one other thing that God provides in abundance: Forgiveness.

About the Author

Author's Website:
https://tyradhodge.blogspot.com/

Tyra Hodge, the founder of Mothers Raising Children Alone, was a homeless mother when God intervened, delivering her spiritually and providing the means for her to attend college. She used her opportunity as a means to change her life. Tyra now holds a Master's degree in Education and is currently working on her Doctoral degree. Currently, Ms. Hodge is an educator specializing with at-risk students. She is a published author of Wounded Daughter Diary, a book about the love of our heavenly father and true forgiveness. She has also written Don't Date Him, a tongue-in-cheek book on dating. In addition to being a full-time mom, wife, and educator, Tyra Hodge is currently working on another book.

www.ingramcontent.com/pod-product-compliance
Lightning Source LLC
Chambersburg PA
CBHW031416290426
44110CB00011B/406